DISSEMINATION OF INFORMATION

DISSEMINATION OF INFORMATION

THOMAS D WILSON FLA
& JAMES STEPHENSON FLA
LECTURERS AT NEWCASTLE UPON TYNE SCHOOL OF LIBRARIANSHIP

PHILOSOPHICAL LIBRARY
NEW YORK

FIRST PUBLISHED 1966 BY PHILOSOPHICAL LIBRARY INC
15 EAST 40TH STREET NEW YORK 16 NY
SET IN LINOTYPE 10 ON 12 POINT BASKERVILLE
AND PRINTED IN GREAT BRITAIN
BY THE CENTRAL PRESS (ABERDEEN) LTD

CONTENTS

CHAPTER ONE
SPECIAL LIBRARIES AND THE
ORGANISATIONS THEY SERVE

THE term 'special library' has always proved difficult to define. Different writers use different criteria and the term has been used to cover so great a variety of libraries that most definitions leave something to be desired. The most satisfactory that we have found is by P Wasserman who defines the special library, in *Library journal* 89 (4) February 1964 797-802, as '. . . an information facility designed to provide access to specialised information and placed within range of and addressed to meet the needs of a special clientele '.

Some idea of the range of organisations which may need special library facilities can be gained by examining the fifteen groups proposed by A T Kruzas in his *Business and industrial libraries in the United States, 1820-1940* (Special Libraries Association, 1965): commercial and industrial firms; newspapers and publishing companies; business and trade associations; scientific societies and institutions; civic-social-religious organisations; historical societies; law firms and associations; public libraries; municipal agencies; state agencies; federal agencies; colleges and universities; museums; hospitals; and miscellaneous and undetermined.

These parent organisations must be studied in some detail. British examples of the above groups can be found in the ASLIB *Directory* and the following information should be sought:

1 Kind of staff employed and their likely information needs; staff hierarchy.

2 Subject interest of the organisation itself and interests of individuals within it.

3 What demand for information is likely from outside, *eg* from members of a society?

4 Channels of communication within the organisation, *eg* internal reports, meetings.

5 Methods used within the organisation to disseminate information other than in 4 above.

FIGURE ONE : THE MAJOR LEVELS OF MANAGEMENT

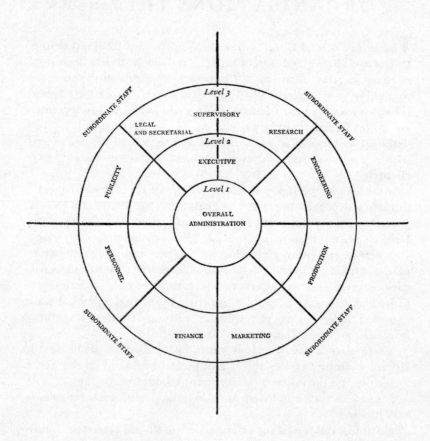

Level	Accountable for
1	Directing main functions
2	Directing supervision of activities
3	Supervising performance of operations

For convenience we can concentrate on three broad groups of organisations: societies and institutions; research organisations; industrial firms.

Societies and institutions: Using the ASLIB *Directory* or *Directory of British associations* (CBD, 1965) select two professional societies. Consult their handbooks and yearbooks to determine:

1 Aims of the society—most likely to be found in charter or bye laws.

2 Educational functions—examination system—special facilities for students.

3 Publications—note any special series such as the Iron and Steel Institute *Special report series*.

4 Information role—library and information services offered; library publications.

5 Professional meetings.

6 Contact and special arrangements with kindred organisations.

Research organisations: in the UK these are chiefly of two types: government research stations and laboratories, and industrial research associations. Reference to recent issues of *Research for industry* (DSIR) will show the range of activities of research associations which are grant-aided. Choose a prominent association, *eg* BISRA, and examine it for the following:

1 Information services: publication of, and access to the report literature of the association; other publications.

2 Range of research topics: the organisation and control of research projects.

3 Application of research results, patents and licences.

4 Contact with other organisations.

An understanding of the organisation of civil research in Great Britain is important in view of recent changes which have been made by legislation. The situation before 1965 is described in the *Trend report* (Cmnd 2171 Oct 1963). The resulting *Science and technology act* (Eliz 2 1965 Ch 4) should be studied. Note that under this act DSIR and its functions have been absorbed by the Department of Education and Science and the Ministry of Technology. Note also the creation of two new research councils.

Industrial firms: it is important to have a clear understanding of the different kinds of industrial organisation. A brief introduction can be found in M K Swift, *Basic business studies*, Book 1 *Commerce*, chapter two ' Owners of businesses ' and chapter three

NB x? indicates borderline interest	Level 3 production management	Engineering designers	Level 3 engineering management	Research designers	Research engineers	Research lab & workshop staff	Level 3 research management	Level 2 management	Level 1 management
General commercial trends								x	x
General technical trends							x	x	x
Technical ideas			x		x		x		
Technical development		x	x	x	x		x		
Commercial development			x					x	x
Contracts and tenders								x	
Market surveys								x	x
Research results (from outside)			x	x	x		x	x	x
Research results (from inside)		x	x					x	x
Advanced technical information			x?	x	x	x	x		
Standards and codes of practice		x		x	x	x			
Workshop & lab manuals	x		x			x			
Trade catalogues	x	x	x			x			
Databooks		x	x	x	x	x			
Bibliographical searching		x?	x?		x		x		
Reports, theses		x?		x	x		x		
Translations		x	x		x		x	x	
Patents		x			x		x	x	x?
Published abstracts				x	x	x	x		
Home made abstracts	x	x	x	x	x	x	x	x	x
Periodicals in own subject field	x	x	x	x	x	x	x		
General periodicals	x	x	x	x	x	x	x	x	x

FIGURE TWO: SHOWING SOME OF THE POSSIBLE INFORMATION REQUIREMENTS OF AN ENGINEERING ORGANISATION

' Public enterprise '. The information demands of the management of commercial undertakings should be clearly understood. Figures one and two in this chapter show the general organisation and information demands which might be expected. Useful organisation charts can be found in A Kent *Specialised information centers* (Spartan Books, 1965).

Descriptions of individual libraries and information services are readily available, *eg* ' BISRA's development and information services' by J Negus, *Steel and coal* 186 (4, 931) January 18 1963 118-121; 'Local access to the aerospace technical literature' by M S Day, ASLIB *Proceedings* 15 (7) July 1963 211-217, a useful survey of the technical information activities of the National Aeronautics and Space Administration; ' CA's information centre (or *Which?*'s library)', by D H Grose, *Assistant librarian* 58 (2) February 1965 26-29; 'The National Referral Center: science and technology in the Library of Congress' by M W McFarland, ASLIB *Proceedings* 16 (8) August 1964 258-268; 'The National Lending Library for Science and Technology, Boston Spa, Yorkshire, England' by V Tortzen, *Libri* 13 (2) 1963 118-126; 'The United Nations' library 1945-1961' by V W Clapp, *Libri* 12 (2) 1962 111-121; and R Hindson 'The dissemination of published information to executives of a major steel group' ASLIB *Proceedings* 17 (1) January 1965 8-22.

The student should compare the purposes for which these services were established. What similarities exist, and what differences? What common services do they offer?

CHAPTER TWO
SOURCES OF INFORMATION

BEFORE discussing the various ways by which information may be disseminated throughout an organisation, it is necessary to pay some attention to the sources of information.

BOOKS

Traditionally books are the major constituents of libraries, but in special libraries their importance has declined, though they are by no means as useless as is sometimes suggested. They remain the repositories of basic information, of facts and data, as in encyclopedias and other reference works, and occasionally present new syntheses, too broad in scope for any other sort of presentation.

The books found in special libraries can be divided into three categories: reference works such as handbooks and tables of data; monographic works within the fields of interest of the organisation; standard textbooks covering the fields of major interest and some fringe subjects. They are all general publications in the sense that they are produced by commercial publishers or by university presses, by societies, and occasionally by industrial concerns who produce handbooks for their own use and then find they are of interest to their customers and other firms.

To their importance as sources of information must be added the fact that in addition to providing data and descriptions of methods, processes and devices, they may be used in literature searching. Many monographs include extensive bibliographies and these may be the first sources to be checked in carrying out a search. They can often provide a starting date for further searching.

PERIODICALS

As books have declined in importance so periodicals have increased. The student should know something of the development of the scientific journal and of the present range of this type of material. D J de S Price has written two useful works on the growth of science and scientific literature, *Science since Babylon* (Yale University Press, 1961) and *Big science, little science* (Yale University Press, 1963). Two articles on the volume of scientific and technical periodical literature are C P Bourne in *American documentation* 13 (2) April 1962 159-168, and C F Gottschalk and W F Desmond in *American documentation* 14 (3) July 1963 188-194.

Periodicals commonly found in special libraries can be divided into the following groups:

Learned journals published by societies and other bodies (*eg Journal of applied mechanics,* published by the American Society of Mechanical Engineers);

'News' journals published by societies, often including technical papers of the review type (*eg Spectrum,* published by the Institute of Electrical and Electronic Engineers);

Learned journals published by commercial publishers (*eg Journal of nuclear energy,* published by Pergamon Press);

Trade journals published by commercial publishers, which cover a very wide range from those which contain mostly technical articles to those which contain chiefly commercial news (*eg Electrical review,* published by Iliffe);

House journals, again a diverse group (*eg* IBM *Journal of research and development,* published by International Business Machines Corporation);

Abstracting and indexing journals, which may be published by government bodies (*eg Nuclear science abstracts,* published by the USAEC); by societies (*eg Chemical abstracts,* published by the American Chemical Society); by commercial publishers (*eg Applied science and technology index,* published by H W Wilson Co); and by co-operative research and development organisations (*eg Copper abstracts,* published by the Copper Development Association);

Review or 'advances' serials, a group that has increased considerably in numbers over recent years (*eg Advances in chemical physics,* published by Interscience).

Examples of these groups should be studied in order to discover what categories of information they contain. It is only by actual examination of journals that one learns of such features as, for example, the reviews of films in *Electrical manufacture,* statistics of units of electricity sold and supplied in *Electricity,* the annual products manufacturers index in *Radio mentor,* or the events diary in many journals which is valuable for advance notice of conferences, or the abstracts on electronic components, materials and techniques in *Electronic components.* These are typical features which can be of use in special library reference and information work and students should examine and make notes on the special features of as many periodicals as possible.

Quite apart from individual features which may be of help to the special librarian, periodical articles constitute a major source of information for the research worker, practising engineer, or manager. The flexibility and immediacy of the medium accounts for the growth not only of periodical literature itself, but also of the guides to this literature in the form of abstracts, indexes and review serials. Such publications are the chief tools of the literature searcher and will be discussed again in chapter eight.

REPORTS

Recent years have seen an almost explosive growth of research report literature, which had its origins in the technological developments provoked at the time of the first world war, but which rose to special prominence in the second world war and has been increasing in volume ever since. J Tallman has described the characteristics of research reports (in *Sci-tech news* 15 (2) Summer 1961 44-46) as follows:

' 1 The report literature is voluminous in the number of titles issued and in the number of agencies involved in their origination . . .

' 2 The reports are heterogeneous and represent a great range in quality in both form and content . . .

' 3 The distribution of reports is often limited . . .

' 4 They are not available from book trade sources, but only through specified government agencies . . .

' 5 They are not usually referenced in conventional bibliographical tools . . . The librarian must become familiar with a whole new set of indexes and procedures.

' 6 There is no union list as to the holdings of reports in designated libraries . . .

' 7 These reports are difficult to handle, once they are acquired . . . Nowadays they are often available only in microcard or microfilm form . . .

14

' 8 Although the reports are the result of national defence sponsorship, they contain a great deal of basic and applied scientific data of use to the public at large. In many cases they are the only source of advanced or specialised information and cannot, therefore, be ignored.'

Some ideas of the extent of report literature can be gained by visiting any public library which is a depository for, say, atomic energy reports or, especially, the National Lending Library for Science and Technology. The student should be familiar with the scope and indexing systems of such tools as *Nuclear science abstracts, Scientific and technical aerospace reports* (STAR), and the new *Government-wide index to federal research and development reports.*

As indicated above, reports are not always easy to obtain. Many American reports can be purchased from the US Clearing House for Federal Scientific and Technical Information, but often approaches must be made to issuing agencies and sometimes even to individual authors. British reports are obtainable through various bodies, including HMSO, the UKAEA and the Ministry of Aviation. Many are security classified and can only be obtained if a ' need to know ' (*eg* because of participation in government contracts) can be established.

Although the importance of reports as sources of information is not to be doubted there is some conflict over their useful length of life. Many are progress reports, often superseded later by a final report on the subject; others deal with minor aspects of such things as the design of specific apparatus; many are reprinted as periodical articles, and some are delivered at conferences, finding their way into conference proceedings. C W J Wilson has discussed the problem of obsolescence of report literature at Harwell in ASLIB *Proceedings* 16 (6) June 1964 200-201.

TRADE LITERATURE

In many special libraries trade literature is an important source of information. This is particularly the case in libraries serving production and design staffs which may be concerned with the purchase of components from other firms, or wish to compare other firms' designs with their own. The major difficulty over trade literature is keeping it up to date, since this involves regular and tedious checking of files. The following references provide basic information: 'The paradoxical trade catalog' by W S Budington in *Special libraries* 46 (3) March 1955 113-117; 'Organising an engineering data file' by A F Gagne in *Machine design* 9 23 Sept 1951 110-116 196; *The treatment of special materials in libraries* by R L Collison (ASLIB, 1955).

CONFERENCE PAPERS

Professional meetings (*ie* conferences, symposia, congresses) produce a wealth of information in the form of papers and subsequent discussion. The number of meetings being held is continuing to grow at a fast rate. Problems are:

1 Lack of information about meetings to be held in the future.
2 Many papers presented at meetings are never published at all.
3 Lack of publicity for published papers and difficulty of bibliographical work involved in tracing them.

Consider each problem:

1 *Lack of information about future meetings*: This is now solved to a certain extent by several publications with which students should be familiar. They are: Union of International Associations *International congress calendar*, an annual publication; UIA 'Calendar' which appears in the UIA journal *International associations; World list of future international meetings*, published monthly by the Library of Congress. It should be realised too that many professional journals try to include regular lists of future national and international meetings in their own subject area. A useful exercise would be to compare the lists of meetings announced in three or four journals concerned with the same subject field.

2 *Papers which are not published*: This is a very serious problem indeed. A selection of papers presented at conferences held in the United States between 1948 and 1950 were surveyed by F Liebesny (*Proc international conference on scientific information*, Washington 1958 1 1959 474-9) who showed that 48.5 percent of the papers presented were never published anywhere.

3 *Lack of publicity for published papers*: Conference papers appear in print in various ways which are fully discussed in UNESCO *Bulletin for libraries* 16 (3 and 4) May-June and July-August 1962 113-126 165-176. Often preprints (*ie* copies of the texts of papers which are printed before the meeting) are the only material which can be obtained for some considerable time. Broadly speaking,

16

published papers appear in one of two ways—as a contribution to a periodical, often without any indication that it was first read as a meeting paper, or collectively with the other conference papers as a separate publication, often with a distinctive title. M L Pflueger contributed a most useful article to *Special libraries* 55 (4) April 1964 200-1 dealing with the bibliographical problems created by conference literature.

Acquisition of published conference papers presents certain problems too. Some are published by the organising body and some by commercial publishers. Handbooks and yearbooks of professional institutions are an important source of information on conference proceedings (see the *Iron and Steel Institute handbook* as an example). Certain publishers too are noted for their work in publishing conference papers and a useful list of conference publications is now being produced by the NLL, *Index of conference proceedings received* No 1 1964. The librarian must also scrutinise the professional press for notes of new conference publications.

Abstracting and indexing services are a means of tracing conference papers. *Engineering index* and *Chemical abstracts* are two good examples of services which do this and they, or other suitable alternatives, should be looked at.

BRITISH PATENTS

This subject must be dealt with in some detail because of the importance of patents in information work. Since patent systems function in much the same way in all countries it is sufficient to understand in detail the British system.

Before commencing a study of patent publications and their information potential it is necessary to understand what patents are and how they are produced. A paper by L J H Haylor ' Scientific information and patents' in ASLIB *Proceedings* 14 (10) October 1962 342-9 will be found to be helpful in this respect. Remember that ' Letters Patent ' say two things: that a named person or body has invented something and that for a specified period the person or body shall have a monopoly in the manufacture, sale and use of the invention. An abbreviated form of Letters Patent is given by C Lees *Institution of Mechanical Engineers proceedings* 169 1955 1210-17. Note that the main purpose of a patent is *not* to reward inventors but to offer inducement to disclose their inventions.

FIGURE THREE : PATENT PROCEDURE

APPLICATION TO PATENT OFFICE

PROVISIONAL PROTECTION

WITHIN TWELVE MONTHS
OF APPLICATION

COMPLETE SPECIFICATION
FILED AT PATENT OFFICE

OFFICIAL SEARCH

WITHIN TWO MONTHS OF NOTICE
AMENDMENT OF SPECIFICATION

WITHIN EIGHTEEN MONTHS
OF APPLICATION

ACCEPTANCE OF SPECIFICATION

DURING THESE STAGES LITTLE INFORMATION IS AVAILABLE. 'OFFICIAL JOURNAL' WILL LIST UNDER SUBJECT, APPLICANT'S NAME AND APPLICATION NUMBER

WITHIN TWENTY ONE MONTHS
OF APPLICATION

SEALING OF PATENT ←— PATENT NOW OPEN TO THE PUBLIC AND COPIES MAY BE PURCHASED FROM PATENT OFFICE

PROVISIONAL PROTECTION ENDS

Patent rights are often misunderstood and the literature on the subject is not very helpful in this respect. These rights entitle the patent owner: to bring an action at law to prevent others putting the invention into use without the permission of the patent holder; to sell the patent outright to another person; to grant licences to others to use the invention.

Patent terminology should be understood by the student and a paper by G H Davison ' Facts concerning patents . . .' in ASLIB *Proceedings* 5 (2) May 1953 101-119 will be found to give good definitions. Make sure that the following terms are understood: application, provisional specification, complete specification, official report, acceptance, sealing, revocation, patent pending, caveat, assignee, patent of addition.

Although there is no need to go into patent procedure very deeply, a knowledge of how the system works is useful. The paper by Lees cited above will be found helpful if read in conjunction with figure three.

For an up to date scale of fees ignore those quoted by Davison (*op cit*) and consult *Applying for a patent,* an annual pamphlet produced by the Patent Office for the guidance of inventors. Note that these fees are on an increasing scale and the total cost of patent protection for 16 years is £183. Note also that these are official fees only, and do not include the cost of inventing borne by the inventor or those charged by patent agents if their services are used.

The essential requirements of a patentable invention should also be grasped and Davison (*op cit*) will help with this.

To exploit patents fully as a source of information, certain bibliographical tools are essential and students should be familiar with them:

1 *Reference index to the classification key and classification conversion table* (Patent Office, 1963). Pay particular attention to the conversion table which is essential in view of the recent changes in the classification.

2 *List of patents in force* . . . Annual.

3 *Index of names of applicants* . . . Annual.

4 *Fifty years subject index, 1861-1910.*

5 *Group allotment index to abridgements of specifications.*

6 *Official journal (patents).* This should be known well. A weekly publication from the Patent Office which is essential for current patent information.

Patent specifications and abridgements of specifications need to be studied most carefully. Note that in the complete specification the claims, which are very important, follow the description and precede the drawings (if any). Make a note of the information found on the first page of the specification—serial number, patentee etc. Look carefully at abridgements and note the amount of information they give. They are an essential tool for current patent information and for retrospective searching.

Availability of patent specifications is dealt with by Davison (*op cit*) and in *Applying for a patent*. Note the system of deposit collections in libraries throughout the country and the deposit account system operated by the Patent Office.

Patent searching: For current information look at the *Official journal* and consider its value to a ' current awareness ' service from the point of view of subject and name approaches. Davison suggests an abstracting service, the abstract cards later forming a classified index. In approach by number no problem exists, but remember for retrospective searching that during the period 1852-1916 there were annual sequences of numbers. For subject searching the *Abridgements* are invaluable.

As an exercise, choose two subjects from the *Reference index to the classification key*. Trace patents dealing with your subjects through the abridgements. Attempt to determine the relevance to the subject of each patent discovered by using the information contained in the abridgement.

Patent classification: Some knowledge of the working of the classification scheme is necessary and a paper by E M Bennett ' Searching classified patent specifications ' ASLIB *Proceedings* 4 (2) May 1952 75-82 will be found useful. Since this paper appeared before the reorganisation of the classification scheme it should be studied in conjunction with the *Reference index to the classification key*.

There has been recent evidence of interest by librarians in applying modern indexing techniques to patents. Co-ordinate indexing seems to have distinct possibilities in this direction, as is shown in B Montague ' Patent indexing by concept co-ordination using links and roles ' *American documentation* 13 (1) January 1962 104-11.

Foreign patents: A catalogue knowledge of the location of sets of foreign patents in this country is not needed but the student should be aware that collections do exist. Davison gives a useful list of locations but J P Lamb in *Commercial and technical libraries* (Allen & Unwin, 1955) is no longer accurate. In this respect see a table given by R C Wilson in *Chemical engineering* 71 (5) March 1964 107 dealing with American patents. He gives another useful table on page 106 indicating the various indexes available for American patents.

STANDARDS

'Standards are documents formulated by agreement, authority or custom of sponsors, to define a product, material, process or procedure, quality, construction, operating characteristics, performance nomenclature and other like facts.' This attempt to define standards is by A S Tayal in 'Standard specifications in libraries' UNESCO *Bulletin for libraries* 15 (4) July-August 1961 203-5, a most useful paper on this little-written-about topic.

Throughout the world there are many standards-issuing bodies, some being governmental organisations others independent bodies. The British Standards Institution is *not* a British government department. Most developed countries in the world have similar institutions to BSI.

As an exercise, choose three countries, other than the United Kingdom, and trace information on their standardisation organisations. Make notes too on the objectives and activities of the International Organisation for Standardisation. A list of those standards organisations which are members of the ISO is given in Tayal (*op cit*).

Most standards are not difficult to trace as the issuing bodies usually produce a handbook or yearbook listing their publications. Examine the BSI *Yearbook* and one similar publication of a foreign standards organisation noting series of standards given and the method of designation used. To supplement their annual lists most organisations issuing standards also produce a periodical giving information on standards, new standards and any that have been withdrawn. Examine copies of BSI *News* and note typical contents.

It is not usual in special libraries to give very full cataloguing and classification treatment to standards, if any such treatment is given at all. Standards are most often asked for specifically by number; the question ' what standards exist on . . .?' is asked only rarely and can usually be answered by a perusal of the yearbooks of the issuing bodies.

The work and publications of the British Standards Institution should be well known, particularly with regard to the services offered for foreign standards. BSI not only makes available for loan from its library many foreign standard specifications, but also maintains stocks of some of them for sale.

A problem often met when dealing with standards is that posed by the library user wanting a British equivalent of a material or process quoted to him according to a foreign standard. Although the librarian cannot be expected to determine equivalents he should be able to produce the publications which will help his reader to make the conversion for himself. The following publications are good examples of tools which can be used in this respect and they, or similar publications, should be known:

1 *Nachschlagewerke stahlschlussel* (1964).

2 *British and foreign specifications for steel castings* (two volumes, British Steel Castings Research Association).

Another problem arises over information on materials produced according to a manufacturer's standard. Such standards are often difficult to trace and frequently impossible to obtain. One publication which is useful in this respect and should be known by the student is N E Woldman *Engineering alloys* (1962).

MICRO MATERIALS

Up to the second world war microfilm was the common form adopted for microstorage of information; but in the post war years other forms have been developed. A useful short description of the different kinds of microforms was given by A Gunther in UNESCO *Bulletin for libraries* 16 (1) January-February 1962 1-21, whilst G H Davison in *Library Association record* 63 (3) March 1961 69-78 treats fully the history and possibilities of microcard and microfiche. Anyone unfamiliar with the different forms of microrecording would be well advised to read these two papers.

The ways in which micro materials assist the dissemination of information are many: reduced storage space, obtaining out-of-print books and other materials, completing sets (particularly periodicals), interlibrary loans, assisting towards self-sufficiency etc. Their great potential in respect of these uses is now fully realised and well summarised in a paper by L S Thompson in *Library trends* 8 (3) January 1960 359-71.

Although the use of microforms in the library does produce certain problems of storage, cataloguing and reading, they are not insurmountable. The solutions to some of them (*eg* storage) are mainly a matter of applied common sense on the part of the librarian, who can obtain good guidance from a paper by H G Bechanan in *Library trends* 8 (3) January 1960 391-406 on the organisation of microforms in the library. Despite the excellence of modern reading machines, full size copies will still be needed at times. These can be produced on most modern reading machines by using contact copying papers. There are, however, other, faster and often completely automatic processes (*eg* xerography) which can be used for this purpose and an evaluation of them can be found in the ALA library technology project *Enlarged prints from library microforms* by W R Hawken (1963).

The major problem connected with micro materials is undoubtedly efficient bibliographical control. A recent survey carried out by the Bibliothèque Nationale and reported in UNESCO *Bulletin for libraries* 19 (3) May-June 1965 139-60 shows that the bibliographical situation with regard to microforms in the major countries of the world is far from satisfactory. Other writers, notably G A Schwegmann in *Library trends* 8 (3) January 1960 380-9 and W Simonton in *Library resources and technical services* 6 (1) Winter 1962 29-40 have written on this topic and suggested various projects which would help. One suggestion is the establishment of a national bibliography of micro materials in each country. Although nothing of this nature is produced in the United Kingdom, the Library of Congress is in the process of gathering information for a register of all master negatives of microfilms in the USA.

This is not to say that the librarian is without bibliographical tools. E M Tilton *Union list of publications in opaque microforms* (1964), The Microcard Foundation *Catalogue of microcard publications* and J Diaz *Guide to microcards in print* (1964) are all useful bibliographies. The Library of Congress and the British Museum both produce a list of newspapers available on microfilm. *Dissertation abstracts,* produced by University Microfilms Inc, lists those American university theses available on microfilm or as xerographic enlargements. Quite apart from these tools

23

there are catalogues of the producers of micro materials. Consult the catalogues of Micro Methods Ltd of Wakefield, for example, to see the range of materials available, particularly periodical sets and out of print books.

It must not be thought that all information is contained in written documents (or reproductions of them); many libraries have as part of their stocks (sometimes a large part), films, illustrations, engineering drawings, gramophone records, diagrammatic materials such as spectra, and even samples of things like plants and fossils. Some of these materials may be obtained through commercial channels, but very often they are the product of the organisation's own activities. In the latter case effective machinery must be established to ensure that material is sent to the library, and once in the library that it can be effectively retrieved. Also important is the archival aspect of some special libraries' activities; care must be taken that historically important materials are preserved.

The student should examine as many examples as possible of the different kinds of material outlined above, discovering: who produces them; how they are obtained; what kind of information they contain; who is likely to require such information; what guides to their contents exist.

Visits to libraries to see how materials are obtained, stored and used will pay dividends.

CHAPTER THREE
METHODS OF DISSEMINATION

We can divide the means of dissemination into two groups:

1 Those directed towards all users (present and potential) of the service: accession lists; periodical article title lists: abstract bulletins.

2 Those directed towards groups of users or individuals: bibliographic surveys; surveys of non-bibliographic information; on-demand bibliographies and surveys; selective dissemination of information; periodical circulation; data sheets; informal conversation, telephone calls.

Rarely will any one library make use of all of these methods; rather it will adopt those which are thought to be of maximum benefit to its clientele. Remember also that they are not watertight compartments; for example, an accession list may be combined with an abstract bulletin and the material collected for the latter may also be used in the preparation of bibliographies.

Accession lists: The accession list is a common feature of libraries of many different kinds, its function being to inform library users of new materials acquired. In special libraries it will include not only books and new periodical titles, but probably the whole range of material acquired: trade literature, micro materials, research reports and the rest. In very large special libraries such an omnibus list may be too bulky and therefore special lists, covering different kinds of material, may be produced: it is common practice to single out research reports for this treatment. The accession list, and all other methods discussed below, must include the parent organisation's own publications as well as those acquired from outside.

Periodical article title lists: This is a reasonably quick method of informing a large number of people of the contents of journals taken by the library. It is sometimes adopted as an alternative to the circulation of periodicals. Format varies. Sometimes the list is arranged in order of journal, with the contents reprinted underneath each title, sometimes it is arranged in subject sequence. The former is faster and useful for those individuals who scan a particular group of journals regularly. The latter takes more time to prepare, but if the library indexes periodical articles it does kill two birds with one stone. It can also serve to draw the attention of users to articles in journals which they would not normally scan. A further alternative is to photocopy the contents lists of journals, but this becomes very expensive if there is a large number of users.

Abstracts bulletins: The reasons for producing an internal abstracts bulletin are not hard to find: commercially available services are often very late in their abstracting; they cover a larger number of journals and are therefore more difficult to scan; they may not include all journals taken by the library; they are general in scope and are not directed towards so specialised a group of users.

The decision to abstract internally, however, must be based firmly upon a need for such a service. Either there should have been a number of requests for a bulletin, or it should be started as an experiment and its usefulness checked by survey at a later date. If periodicals are not circulated the bulletin acts as an alternative means of disseminating information of their contents. It is unwise to spend too much time on the actual abstracting: indicative abstracts will suffice, and if already given in the periodical they can just be copied. An exception to this occurs in large organisations where the library is serving widely scattered users. Under these circumstances, informative abstracts may be worthwhile as they may cut down requests for photocopies or loans of articles which are not really apposite. Further information on abstracting is given in chapter seven.

The foregoing lists may be combined into one publication—a library bulletin. The advantage of a composite bulletin is that it reduces the number of library publications which a conscientious user must scan. A possible disadvantage is that it may be extremely bulky.

Whatever the type of library publication developed, certain factors must be considered carefully: its cost to the organisation, and whether it is worth it; what production methods are to be used (see chapter four); what arrangement and layout should be adopted; is an index to be produced; is a bulletin really necessary?

The type of entry which gives the cleanest layout on the page is best. It is difficult for a librarian to deviate from a standard catalogue entry but the aim of this type of publication is to convey information quickly and it is important to ' engineer ' the entries so that this is achieved. The *Battelle technical review* abstracts section, with its emphasis of ' clue-words ', is interesting in this respect. Alphabetic-subject arrangement and numbering of items is common and a tear-off request form which the user can send to the library requesting particular items is useful and can give some indication of how well the bulletin is used.

Whether an index is to be produced depends entirely upon how the publication is used. If it is kept for personal reference, then an index is useful and, if alphabetic-subject arrangement is used, production is relatively mechanical. Indeed, the English Electric information department produces an index to its bulletin by computer, as does the Burrough's Corporation, see *Special libraries* 54 (6) July-August 1963 345-349.

Is a bulletin really necessary, or will other methods be more useful? It is necessary here to compare the efficiency of a bulletin, which will go to all users, with the more selective methods discussed below. Only an assessment of user needs and preferences will answer this question. Library bulletins are discussed, with illustrations in L J Strauss and others, *Scientific and technical libraries* (Wiley, 1964); K G Blair has made a comparison of engineering library bulletins in *Special libraries* 52 (4) April 1961 175-182, and a bulletin for company reports is described by F E McKenna in *Special libraries* 56 (5) May-June 1965 318-322.

Information may be disseminated on a more limited and specialised basis to groups and individuals. The methods discussed below are not intended to be comprehensive, and indeed, could not be so, since there are so many variations—they are simply indicative of the varieties.

Bibliographic surveys: By this is meant the literature survey on a particular topic prepared for an individual or a research team. Thus a group carrying out research on, say, high-temperature ceramics for nuclear applications, may express a need for a regular literature survey. The aim of this kind of survey is not simply to list current articles but to draw together those on common aspects, and to present their methods, conclusions etc in a co-ordinated form. Obviously anyone attempting such a service must have some subject knowledge but good work of this kind is being done by people who have acquired all their subject knowledge ' on the job '.

Surveys of non-bibliographic information: This is a cumbersome name for a publication which is directed towards groups of users (*eg* in sales and management), who are interested in information on new materials and new products in economic information and who do not wish to spend time in searching in newspapers, trade literature and journals. As with other methods mentioned, an obvious need must be expressed before embarking upon the production of surveys of this kind as they are time-consuming if done well.

On-demand bibliographies and surveys: As well as being prepared on a continuing basis surveys and bibliographies are often prepared on a particular topic as a result of an information request. This may lead to requests for a continuing service and in any case the methods of preparation are identical. Literature searching is discussed in chapter eight.

Selective dissemination of information: This is the provision of single items of information to individuals. There are four elements in the operation of such a system: a list of individual subject interests; a regular scanning of incoming information and comparison with those subject interests; a method of informing individuals of items of interest; a ' feed-back ' system, whereby the library is informed as to the usefulness of the information supplied and any changes in the users' interests.

Librarians have operated such systems on a manual basis for some time, but the most significant development in recent years has been the use of computers and punched card equipment to mechanise the procedures. The leader in this field was H P Luhn whose report (available from IBM) *Selective dissemination of new scientific information with the aid of electronic processing equipment* (1959), also in *American documentation* 12 (2) April 1961 131-138, was the original paper on the subject. Basically the system operates as follows:

1 Each user submits a ' profile ' of his interests—usually a list of indexing terms taken from the standard list used in the system. This profile is transferred to computer storage on magnetic tape

via punched cards or any other appropriate input medium. The user's departmental address is included.

2 Incoming information is indexed and similarly stored on magnetic tape.

3 The computer compares the two inputs at predetermined intervals. Where sufficient terms on the user profile and document profile match, the computer then prints out the details of the document on to two punched cards—an information card, which incorporates a tear-off strip request note and a 'response card'.

4 The user retains the information card for his own files, sending the request strip to the library if he wishes to read the document. He also returns the response card upon which he notes the degree of interest which he has in the document.

5 The library can now take action on both the cards, information from the response card being used to update the user-profile and ensure a more efficient service. Further information on SDI is to be found in ASLIB *Proceedings* 14 (12) October 1962 473-503, and in *Automation and scientific communication: short papers of the* ADI *annual meeting* (American Documentation Institute, 1963) 69-70.

Periodical circulation: The thorny question of whether or not to circulate periodicals, and the mechanisms for doing so are well dealt with in library literature, *eg* ASLIB *Proceedings* 6 (3) August 1954 146-150, *Special libraries* 45 (9) November 1954 371-375 and *Special libraries* 53 (9) November 1962 537-540. The bases for decision are fourfold: the number of people to be served; their physical location relative to the library; the number of journals involved; and the comparative costs of circulation and the alternatives.

The great fault with periodical circulation is the time it takes. Therefore if many people are involved the process defeats itself. Limits are usually arbitrary but there seems to be little point in trying to circulate a periodical to more than twelve to fifteen individuals. Purchase of duplicates to overcome this limitation quickly becomes expensive. Apart from the slowness of service, circulation also introduces a very real danger of loss and mutilation. Nor is it worthwhile to circulate periodicals to individuals who have quick and easy access to the library. Regular scanning of a number of periodicals need take very little time and could usefully draw the user's attention to journals he does not normally scan. So far as widely scattered users are concerned one of the alternatives to circulation, such as a bulletin, is the answer.

The work involved in periodical circulation is very time-consuming and therefore costly. Most special libraries take a considerable number of journals and it is not unusual to find a member of staff fully employed on work of this kind.

There is no cheap way of informing users of the contents of periodicals. The alternatives to circulation are: title lists discussed above (also expensive); abstract bulletins (more informative and more costly); and drastic though it seems, display of periodicals in the library without further service.

The last is undoubtedly the cheapest, but limitation of a service in this manner is unlikely to appeal to users, although it would probably work in a small library. One major disadvantage is that unless members of the library staff scan journals they may miss information of value: if they do scan then they might as well scan purposefully and offer a positive service.

Data sheets: There are times when particular tasks require information on, for example, properties of materials, or economic information on foreign countries. If such information is intended to be of use to a number of people, some libraries make a practice of issuing a regular series of data sheets. A major service of this kind is offered by the UKAEA and its publications made available to the public *eg Zirconium data manual*, compiled by B J Seddon, TRG report 108 (R) (HMSO, 1962). The development of 'information centres' in the USA has led to the production of data sheets as a major part of the service *eg* those of the Electronic Properties Information Center.

Informal conversation, telephone calls: If a special librarian is to do his job properly then he must spend a considerable part of his time talking to people, finding out what they are doing. Not only will he learn much of value, but he will also be able to pass on information culled from journals, and, not unusually, to and from members of different research teams. It follows that informal conversations and telephone calls can often be a potent means of disseminating information and they serve the further functions of keeping the librarian informed of what is happening in his organisation and, importantly, showing that he is interested in the activities of others.

CHAPTER FOUR
LIBRARY PUBLICATIONS

IN an article in UNESCO *Bulletin for libraries* 16 (2) March-April 1962 64-72 J H Shera describes documentation as a means of escaping from ' poverty in the midst of intellectual abundance' and continues 'documentation . . . may be regarded as a theory of librarianship that is dedicated to the exploration of new ways for improving the utility of recorded knowledge '. Although Shera is concerned in this article with new ways of exploiting existing information it should be remembered that information workers use established techniques which have existed for many years. These techniques include the production of secondary publications which have documentation as their basic purpose, *ie* making the information contained in primary publications more acceptable by reorganisation to suit the needs of the user.

The great quantity of literature, particularly scientific literature, produced nowadays demands some form of condensation. Even in highly specialised fields no one person can hope to have available and have time to read and use all the literature that exists on the subject. In an attempt to alleviate the situation abstracts, indexes and digests are produced.

The publications of the information department are of the librarian's creating; their quality and effect are his responsibility and to some extent he will be judged by their success. Various kinds of publications are issued by information departments, for example abstract bulletins, information digests, bibliographies. Although it is unlikely that any one library will issue all those kinds listed in the ASLIB *Handbook* (on page 373) it is usual to produce some of them, depending on the needs of the users of the library. A reading of other chapters of this guide, particularly chapters three and eight, will show that not all library publications have the same circulation. For example abstract bulletins are circulated widely whereas bibliographies, being usually the response to a specific request, have a more restricted circulation. Since the cost of producing these publications is usually very important, the number of copies required will be the main factor in determining the methods used to reproduce them.

Once publications have been established they should not be allowed to continue indefinitely without periodic assessment. By using a combination of direct inquiries, user surveys and checks on loan requests which these publications create, their value to the library's clientele can be judged. In this way publications can be remodelled to suit changing interests and weaknesses removed; alternatively they can cease if the original demand for them has disappeared.

Of the publications produced in special libraries, accessions lists, catalogues and short lists of publications are probably the most common. They should be produced in as simple a fashion as possible, have an uncomplicated layout and contain only essential information. Entries in such lists for books and pamphlets need contain nothing more than the author, title and date of publication, and the title, number and date would be sufficient in entries for standards. Compilation of this kind of list presents no major problems provided they are prepared on a regular basis. The information for the lists is gathered as items are received and is cumulated at intervals. Bibliographies should have the same layout as accessions lists and catalogues and little, if any, extra bibliographical detail is necessary. Annotations in bibliographies are of doubtful value since the object of compiling such a list is usually to discover only what exists on a subject. Bibliographies extending to several pages are probably best arranged by subject and very extensive ones will require indexing. Short bibliographies can be conveniently arranged by author. T K S Iyengar in *Indian librarian* 14 (4) March 1960 165-9 describes the mechanics of compiling a bibliography.

The other group of publications produced in special libraries are those that contain facts other than bibliographic details *eg* abstracts bulletins, commercial bulletins etc. These too are issued frequently so that the information they contain is always current. For some classes of information such as commercial information, it may be desirable to issue daily bulletins. The important difference between this group of publications and that mentioned previously is that whereas the former lists publications the latter is concerned with information and could include any source of information such as trade literature, newspapers etc. The layout of this kind of bulletin requires considerable care. It is essential that headings should stand out from the remainder of the text, and undue compression of the print on the page should be avoided. Subject arrangement is usually adopted, and for extensive bulletins indexes are needed. Some good examples of layout can be found in *Scientific and technical libraries* by L J Strauss and others (Wiley, 1964). Although the bulletin is the normal method of issuing abstracts, there is a good case sometimes for issuing abstracts separately. The recipient of separate abstracts can thereby keep only those concerned with his subject, without all the unrelated abstracts as he would have to do with a bulletin. The case for and against individual abstract publication is discussed by W R Moss in ASLIB *Proceedings* 11 (4) April 1959 102-5.

A more recent development among library publications is the contents list, the copying and reproducing, either selectively or completely, of titles of articles in current issues of periodicals. This can be done either by direct photocopying, photocopying in conjunction with a duplicator, or typing masters or stencils for duplication. The method chosen depends on facilities and machinery available and on the number of people to whom the list is to be circulated. These lists are produced as a ' current-awareness ' service and are of little permanent value. The cheapest method of reproduction is, therefore, to be recommended. Commercially produced services, such as *Current contents* are now available and some of these should be known and their value assessed.

The presentation of the information in a library publication is very important since this can affect its reception by the user. Good presentation is an aid to reading and bad presentation can be a barrier. Wherever possible a standard list of subject headings should be used and those headings should appear prominently on the printed page. Cross references should be avoided wherever possible, entries being duplicated under different headings if necessary. A serially numbered sequence in a long publication is helpful to the user who wishes to request the original. Rules on spacing, margins, use of upper and lower case, underlining, abbreviations etc should be established. These are best recorded in a rule book or house style manual, together with examples, to maintain consistency in presentation in all publications. Many British standards will be found helpful in relation to the presentation of information *eg* BS 1629 : 1950 on bibliographical references. A list of the most pertinent can be found in ASLIB *Handbook* 383-5. Tables and diagrams need special care and equipment to reproduce them. They are expensive to produce but can be worthwhile if they transmit the information effectively. G W Thomas in *Information and its dissemination*: *report of the summer meeting of the Institute of Petroleum* (1961) 57-74 claims that ' effective presentation cuts publication costs, facilitates information retrieval and contributes in no small way to the progress of our science and technology '. Although he was concerned in this paper with the technical report and the technical paper, most of his remarks are valid for library publications too. Note particularly his remarks on the reproduction of graphs, histograms and charts.

It will be apparent from the foregoing that no one method of documentary reproduction will be suitable for all information department publications. Many copies of an abstract bulletin will be required quickly and therefore a rapid, fairly cheap method of reproduction is needed; but only a small number of copies of a bibliography will be required and in this case a process suitable for economic production of small editions will be best. The process chosen for any publication should give good, readable copies and the finished publication should be as attractive as economic considerations permit. It is not proposed to discuss in this guide the various processes which can be used to reproduce library publications. Short, but adequate, descriptions of the processes can be found in H R Verry *Document copying and reproduction processes* (1960). Concentrate on processes which are commonly used *ie* reflex, diazo, diffusion-transfer, verifax, thermography, xerography and spirit, stencil and offset duplicating. It is extremely important to note the advantages and disadvantages of each process and its suitability for the production of publications. The suitability of a process should be judged by the following factors:

1 Library publications are mainly textual, although allowance must be made for occasional illustrations.

2 Cost. Most publications have a limited life and the cheapest method consistent with quality required should be used.

3 Required quality of copies.

4 Size limits of copies and originals (sometimes).

5 Preparation of originals from which copies are to be made.

6 Urgency of publication.

The most important factor governing the choice of a process is usually that of cost, especially in view of the impermanent nature of many of the publications. Process costs are considered very carefully by Verry (*op cit*) 189-214. Note his tables, especially table IV 'Reproduction methods—some comparisons and costs'. The costs quoted are slightly inaccurate by present day estimates but they do still serve as a comparison. An article by K Gillespie in *Office magazine* (104) August 1962 684-708 is useful for advice on process selection, although it is limited to photocopying methods.

There is much interest at present among librarians in the use of machines to produce indexes. Although these developments belong to the chapters on information retrieval they should be remembered in connection with library publications. It is not impossible that certain publications (*eg* abstract bulletins) will be controlled and produced by machine in the future, as indexes can be at present. C F Cayless and others describe in *Library Association record* 66 (10) October 1964 439-42 a successful experiment at AWRE on the use of punched cards to produce multiple copies of an index to the UDC. The machinery used in the experiment is discussed by R E Coward in the *Library Association record* 67 (2) February 1965 50-1.

Occasionally, information workers may be required to produce or assist in the production of house journals, although such publications are probably better done by journalists. If such a task is obligatory then good advice can be found in a paper by E N Simons in ASLIB *Proceedings* 11 (4) April 1959 87-93.

It is sometimes necessary for the special librarian to organise his own documentary reproduction unit in the absence of suitable facilities elsewhere in his parent organisation. The establishment of such a unit needs great care, particularly with regard to the purchase of the most suitable machinery and the employment of workers who may be classed as manual or industrial. Verry (*op cit*) should be used as a reference source should such a unit have to be established. An article by F Donker Duyvis in UNESCO *Bulletin for libraries* 14 (6) November-December 1960 241-59 will also prove valuable as a reference source on this topic.

CHAPTER FIVE: COPYRIGHT

I T will be obvious from a reading of other chapters of this guide that much copying needs to be done in information work to make the service successful. Users of information services usually have little time to go to other libraries to consult books and periodicals and, what is more important, they frequently need published information in the laboratory, workshop or office as an essential part of their work. The fact that the progress of science was being impeded due to scientists not having access to scientific information was forcibly made at the Royal Society scientific information conference in 1948. This was felt to be due, to a large extent, to the then existing copyright legislation. As a result of this conference the *Royal Society fair copying declaration* was produced. This declaration is a statement by certain publishers of scientific journals to the effect that their publications could be copied without infringement of copyright provided that certain conditions are observed. These conditions closely resemble those in our present copyright legislation, therefore the declaration, although it still exists, has less significance now for information workers.

'Copyright is not a natural right but an artificial creation, which in English law has been built up irregularly to deal with particular contingencies' (from *Journal of documentation* 14 (2) June 1958 46). 'Copyright was and still is intended to protect the author against use of his labours publicly by others for profit without sharing those profits with the author' (from *College and research libraries* 17 (4) July 1956 301). These two quotations show, probably as well as any others, what copyright is and why it exists. Even though copyright may appear to be somewhat nebulous as a possession, adequate provisions are made in our legislation for its protection. The term of copyright is the lifetime of the author plus fifty years. Items published after the author's death have copyright protection for fifty years from the year of publication.

Despite the fact that much copying is done in libraries, often apparently contrary to the regulations, information workers should understand what is legally permitted. The copying of any document is governed by the *Copyright Act* of 1956 (4 & 5 Eliz 2 Ch 74) and various regulations made in statutory instruments. The two sources for reference on copyright are the Act itself and *The Copyright Act 1956* by D H M Davies (Sweet and Maxwell, 1957). A detailed knowledge of the provisions of the legislation does not fall within the syllabus of this paper, but a broad understanding of what they are and how they affect the dissemination of information is necessary.

Generally speaking the following can be freely copied:

1 Sections of a publication which can be shown to be not a substantial part of the publication *eg* single pages copied to complete another imperfect copy.

2 An unpublished document of which a copy is kept in a public institution where it is open to public inspection, provided it is more than one hundred years old and the author has been dead for fifty years.

3 Non-copyright materials; mainly publications originating in other countries and not granted protection under British law *eg* Russian and Chinese. Does not apply to countries of the British Commonwealth and certain other countries (see *Statutory instrument 1957 number 1524*).

4 Published works, the period of copyright protection of which has expired.

5 Any work, provided the permission of the copyright holder has been obtained.

6 Any publication provided it is fair dealing for certain defined purposes *eg* private study or research. This is a most confusing provision which J Woledge in *Journal of documentation* 14 (2) June 1958 50-2 bravely attempts to clarify.

In addition the copyright of texts is not infringed by the making of copies by a librarian under certain conditions, which vary according to whether the copy is made for an individual or for another library. When the copy is made for an individual the following conditions apply:

1 The library making the copy must not be established for

profit. By implication libraries of industrial firms, although not profit making in themselves, are excluded, although the legislation does not specifically say so.

2 The recipient of the copy must sign a declaration to the effect that he has not been previously supplied with a copy by any librarian and that the copy will be used only for private study or research.

3 Only one copy of an item can be supplied to one person.

4 Only one article can be copied from a particular periodical part and only a ' reasonable proportion ' of a non-periodical publication. There is no definition of what is a ' reasonable proportion '.

5 Persons receiving copies must pay a sum equivalent to the cost of making them and this sum is to include a charge for ' overheads '.

6 Unless the item to be copied is from a periodical, copying can only be done if the librarian does not know and cannot, after reasonable enquiry, ascertain who the copyright holder is. In some libraries the responsibility for locating the copyright holder and getting his permission to copy, is the reader's.

Where one library copies anything for another library the conditions applying are:

1 Both libraries must be of the non-profit making kind or make their books available to the public free of charge.

2 No declaration is needed.

3 Only one copy may be supplied unless the first has been lost or destroyed.

4 Payment must be made for the copy by the receiving library.

5 No restriction on the extent of the copy.

Apart from tidying up the existing copyright situation the 1956 Act for the first time covered the typographical arrangement of a published edition. In this case the typographical arrangement of a particular edition of a book has copyright protection even though the book itself (*ie* the text) may have no protection if the term of copyright has expired.

The existing copyright legislation places librarians in a most unenviable position. The librarians of non-profit making organisations are obliged to observe the regulations conscientiously and this inevitably inhibits their ability to disseminate information as deeply as they would probably wish. To collect declarations from readers, keep accounts of the charges for photocopies etc not only takes up the librarian's valuable time but also irritates readers and it is debatable whether or not it does much to protect the interests of the copyright holder. The librarian of a non-profit making organisation feels that he is prevented by the regulations from producing 'contents lists' and the like which he would probably wish to do.

The position of the industrial librarian is even less defined than that of the librarian of a non-profit making institution. A reading of Woledge (*op cit*) suggests that much of the copying done by the industrial librarian in connection with abstracts bulletins, information digests etc could be claimed as fair dealing. Translations likewise could be claimed as fair dealing. Industrial librarians, however, inevitably find it necessary to undertake photocopying of books and periodicals on a large scale because of the needs of their users. Making microcopies and possibly enlargements from microfilm of copyright material could, under certain circumstances, be deemed fair dealing but in other circumstances could be claimed to be an infringement of copyright. The position of the industrial librarian is far from satisfactory but the lack of prosecutions seems to suggest that copyright holders are not unduly concerned about librarians making full use of their copyright materials, though that should not be taken as an exemption from the copyright laws.

CHAPTER SIX
THE LANGUAGE BARRIER

Any attempt to disseminate information in depth on a narrow subject will inevitably bring to the disseminator the problem of language. It is common practice in special libraries to collect foreign language materials both to keep abreast of developments in the subject in other countries and because many outstanding publications appear in languages other than English. The acquisition of foreign publications has its own problems but the major ones, as far as this book is concerned, lie in the use of the information they contain.

The problems created by language in the dissemination of information can be listed as:

1 The number of languages in use throughout the world. J E Holmstrom in ASLIB *Proceedings* 14 (12) December 1962 413-25 estimates that thirty-five to fifty languages contain significant amounts of scientific and technical publications. The accessibility to foreign scientists of information published in some of these languages is very low, and Holmstrom attempts to show this by means of a quantitative representation.

2 Variation in the use of particular languages according to the branch of science concerned. Again Holmstrom produces some interesting figures. For example, two thirds of the world's engineering literature is published in English. The implied problem is that created when one attempts to disseminate information in two subject fields where the language used most for publication is not the same for both subjects (NB the increasing importance of Russian and the probable importance of Chinese in the future).

3 Ability to read foreign languages. Inability to read any language other than one's own mother tongue means the loss of an ever increasing amount of information; the ability to search for and find pertinent information on a subject is governed, to a great extent, by the language knowledge of the searcher. This applies to information workers as well as to scientists and technologists.

For a full treatment of the problems created by languages read Holmstrom (*op cit*) and *The foreign language barrier in science and technology* by C W Hanson (ASLIB, 1962).

Methods of overcoming the language barrier should be considered :

1 Widespread use of an easily learned language applicable to all scientific subjects. Ideally this is probably the best solution provided scientists and technologists can be persuaded to learn such a language and provided publishers use it for scientific publications. Remember that an international scientific language exists to some extent in the form of signs, symbols, chemical formulae etc. An artificial language suitable for scientific communication exists, known as *Interlingua* and its possibilities should be considered. It is described by A Gode in *Journal of dental medicine* 11 (2) April 1956 108-17, and a paper by F F Cleveland in *The American scientist* 47 (3) September 1959 403-12 explains the language with text printed in English and Interlingua.

2 More language instruction for scientists and technologists to enable them better to determine the value of items of foreign literature and thereby ease the strain on existing translation facilities. A perusal of technical college prospectuses will reveal many courses specifically designed for this purpose. As yet there is little evidence of their effect.

3 Improvement in the supply of translations. Much has been done in recent years to make translations of technical information more widely available. Three developments need to be studied :

a) *Cover-to-cover translations*: *ie* complete translations into English of foreign periodical parts as they are published. Much of this work is being done by societies, institutions and research associations, although some commercial publishers produce some too, notably Consultants Bureau Inc. *Stal* and *Machines and tooling* are good examples of cover-to-cover translations and the student would be well advised to examine as many examples as possible. Note the translation agency, the subscription, and the time taken to produce the translation after the appearance of the original.

b) *Co-operation*: two methods are in current use—the formation of a pool of translations from which copies can be purchased or borrowed, and secondly, establishment of a central index of translations which have been made and are available for consultation. The commonwealth index of translations maintained by

ASLIB is well known and is an example of the second method, as is the European translations centre at Delft (for information on the centre see *Revue internationale de documentation* 30 (2) May 1963 51-4). An example of a pooling scheme should be known *eg* the British Iron and Steel Industry Translation Service which is organised by The Iron and Steel Institute.

c) *Machine translations*: *ie* the use of computers, reading and printing machines to translate text automatically from one language to another. Although much research remains to be done in this field, acceptable translations can be produced now. Detailed knowledge of machine translation is probably outside the scope of this paper but a knowledge of the problems involved and the possibilities of its use should be obtained. Papers which will prove particularly useful in this respect are by D Y Panov in *Impact of science on society* 10 (1) 1960 16-25; E Delavenay UNESCO *Bulletin for libraries* 13 May 1959 105-9; S Ceccato *Information storage and retrieval* 2 (3) December 1964 105-58 and S Ceccato and others *International conference on machine translation held at the National Physical Laboratory 1961* papers 30 and 31.

Most organisations making a serious attempt to disseminate information have some arrangement for the production of translations of information in foreign languages. The organisation will either employ translators or use outside agencies or a combination of both. When making visits to special libraries the student should pay particular attention to the system used and note the qualifications of any translator employed. In most localities translation agencies exist and will usually supply details of services offered. Note also that many public libraries maintain lists of translators who are prepared to do freelance work. One of the major problems connected with production of translations within an organisation is that of cost. Translators are expensive to employ and no one organisation could hope to have sufficient translators to cover all the languages likely to be asked for. The economics of producing translations have been dealt with by F Liebesny in ASLIB *Proceedings* 10 (5) May 1958 115-23. The physical preparation of the translation, after the translator has finished with it, often falls to the librarian. Although there is little difference between the production of translations and the production of other kinds of text, two papers by M Wright and J B Reed in ASLIB *Proceedings* 13 (9)

September 1961 228-37 are worthy of consultation. Most of the remarks in chapter four of this guide concerning the production of information department publications apply to the production of translations too.

CHAPTER SEVEN
ABSTRACTS AND ABSTRACTING

Since the beginning of the nineteenth century abstracts have been used by scientists. Now, millions are produced each year to act as retrieval media and current-awareness tools. Basically, abstracts are read to save some of the time it would take to read the originals; often an abstract can be used altogether in lieu of the original, depending on the needs of the user and the quality of the abstract. Most abstracts appear in secondary journals (*ie* abstracting journals), and in abstract bulletins prepared by librarians. Also it is common practice in many periodicals to include an abstract with the original text. Usually this kind of abstract is prepared by the author and is known as an author abstract.

According to a definition given in the UNESCO *International conference on scientific abstracting report* (1951) an abstract is ' a summary of a publication or article accompanied by an adequate bibliographical description to enable the publication or article to be traced '. The key word in this definition is ' summary ' which should be taken to mean a summary of the important part of the original, the unimportant parts or those which are mere repetitions of existing knowledge being ignored in the abstract. The UNESCO report also defines the two kinds of abstract, indicative and informative. A comparison of the definitions of indicative and informative abstracts will show that the informative is nearer to the original definition of an abstract. The informative summarises the original whereas the indicative discusses the original and is really an extension of the library annotation. An examination of any abstracting journal will show that the abstracts they contain are of these two types and that in many journals both kinds are included.

A term which has appeared in literature on abstracting in recent years is ' auto-abstract '. This does not indicate a new kind of abstract; but a new method of producing them. Auto-abstracts are produced with the aid of a computer.

44

An answer to the often asked question ' what information do users expect to get from abstracts?' can be found in *Laboratory practice* 13 (9) September 1964 815. According to this article, a scientist expects an abstract to tell him: that someone has published a paper on a certain subject; what the paper is about; the address of the author.

This is an oversimplified answer to a difficult question, but the article is useful because it expresses the view of the scientist. The address of the author should not be necessary if an efficient library service is available. Sir Alfred Egerton gives a fuller and probably more typical statement of the scientist's attitude to abstracts in *Royal Society scientific information conference report* (1948) 344-7. All writers on this subject agree that abstracts must appear soon after the publication of the original and that the time lag between the publication of the original and the abstract governs, to some extent, the usefulness of the abstract.

The abstract should:

1 Be reasonably up to date.

2 Inform the user of the contents of a paper and help him to decide whether or not he needs to read the original.

3 Be fit to be used as a secondary source of information in information retrieval systems, including abstracting journals.

The abstract should not:

1 Lack clarity.

2 Omit vital information.

3 Be inaccurate.

The published abstracting services have, in recent years, been the subject of research. Much of this research has been concerned with the coverage of the services and the quality of the abstracts. M H Smith in a paper in *International conference on scientific information proceedings* 1 1958 321-50 states that the coverage of an abstracting service should be ' all the published and unpublished information within the field it claims to cover '. This would be impossible for most services, particularly with regard to unpublished materials, and an examination of some of them will reveal restrictions on subject area covered and selection of materials for inclusion. It should be remembered that some information published in journals is repetitive and can, in all probability, be excluded from an abstracting service. Another paper by S Herner (*ibid* 408-27) attempts to determine the degree of subject slanting, *ie* difference in content, structure and emphasis, accorded to the abstracts of certain papers in abstracting journals. Two interesting points emerge:

1 Where an author abstract exists, use is generally made of it in the preparation of abstracts for publication by abstracting services. There is therefore little subject slanting when this is done.

2 Where original abstracts are prepared there is no appreciable subject slanting.

The implication of Herner's findings is that all major abstracting services produce much the same kind of abstract for a particular paper and co-operative abstracting seems possible.

The student should attempt to evaluate some abstracting services in a subject field known to him using Herner's and Smith's methods. *A guide to the world's abstracting and indexing services, in science and technology* published by the National Federation of Science Abstracting and Indexing Services, and *Index bibliographicus* can be used to trace abstracting services.

It is common practice for special libraries to produce their own abstracts and to issue them either singly or collectively in a bulletin. Careful planning of such a service is necessary. The first consideration in establishing such a service is the writing of the abstracts. An article on the writing of abstracts by C K Arnold in the *Institute of radio engineers transactions on engineering writing and speech* EWS —4 (3) December 1961 summarises a good abstract by stating ' your abstract must be a self-contained unit, a complete report in miniature . . . the abstract that cannot stand on its own feet independently must be either rewritten or will fail to perform its job '. H Borko and S Chatman in *American documentation* 14 (2) April 1963 149-60 attempt to produce criteria for abstracts by means of a survey of instructions to abstractors issued by one hundred and thirty abstracting agencies. The interpretation by Borko and Chatman of these instructions should be carefully studied; similarly, the section of their paper dealing with the form of the abstract. Note carefully that an informative abstract should discuss the contents of a paper whereas the indicative abstract should discuss the paper itself. More practical advice on the writing of abstracts is given by W Ashworth in ASLIB *Handbook* 346-53. Note his list of faults to be avoided *eg* unnecessary words, long words etc. Abstractors should beware of the dangers of undue condensation

46

of information in abstracts. It has been shown quite clearly by W A Freedman in STWE *Review* 5 (3) 1958 18-20 that reading speed is reduced according to the degree of compaction of the information. Before establishing an abstracting service certain questions should be answered:

1 How frequently are abstracts to be published?

2 Which users are intended to benefit most? Is the service aimed at any particular kind of user? This may require a survey of users' needs.

3 What foreign language materials are to be included?

4 Who is to do the abstracting?

5 Are books and other materials to be included as well as periodical articles?

With regard to the employment of abstractors it is stated in the *Royal Society scientific information conference report* (1948) 135 that an abstractor should 'have a general scientific background, knowledge of languages and an acquaintance with the field covered'. People with all these qualifications are rare and it may be necessary to accept an abstractor with fewer qualifications than those given above. Ashworth (*op cit*) 353 prefers abstracting to be done by the information officer, although he does recognise the value of assigning the work to subject specialists not employed in the information department.

The reproduction of abstract bulletins is dealt with in chapter four of this guide, together with other kinds of information department publications. It is enough to restate here that they should be reproduced in such a way that they follow quickly on the publication of the original.

CHAPTER EIGHT: FINDING
AND MEETING USERS' NEEDS

AN information service provided without due attention to the needs of users is obviously no information service at all, and the special librarian should be fully aware of the main techniques necessary for discovering what his users want. These techniques can be divided into: observation of the types of requests made by users; investigatory techniques.

The types of requests made can be summarised as follows:

1 Demands for specific documents; the commonest kind of demand, necessitating an adequate collection of bibliographical reference works for ensuring accurate references.

2 Demands for specific data; properties, formulae etc requiring data books in the relevant subject fields.

3 Retrospective searches; the emphasis here is upon 'all relevant references', and a good collection of abstracting and indexing services is essential.

4 Current-awareness demands; the chief requirement for which is a good collection of current periodicals which the user may search himself plus, perhaps, a selective dissemination service run by the library.

5 Exhaustive search demands; an extension of 3 above, usually required when the user needs to know that something definitely does *not* exist, as in patent searches.

6 Searches for research ideas; can only be carried out by the user himself, and often lead to other demands.

While the gradual development of library services to answer the demands outlined above is common, it is often of value to undertake studies in order to discover whether or not the library is serving its users adequately and what kind of services they need. To this end there are a number of techniques which can be used:

1 *Field study*: a lengthy task from the point of view of the observer, but with the advantage that it need consume no addi-

tional time on the part of the user. The technique is simply to observe the way in which a task is carried out, *eg* the way in which a user coming into the library sets about searching for information. The task observed may be of any size, but obviously, from the point of view of limiting the time taken to complete the study, it is important to use this method only for narrowly defined tasks.

2 *Case study*: in the field of information work the commonest way of carrying out a case study is by using diaries in which users record at specific time intervals what they are doing by way of gathering or using information. This method consumes a fair amount of the user's time, and because of the difficulties involved in remembering to fill in the diary due to pressure of other work, or being away from the office or laboratory, is open to error. Simply using the diary may in fact alter needs, since it is, in part, a process of self-analysis. The classic example of this method is Professor J D Bernal's investigation for the Royal Society scientific information conference and published in the conference *Report* (1948) 589-637. Other investigations include: ' Methods by which research workers find information ' by R M Fishenden in *Proceedings of the international conference on scientific information* (National Research Council, 1959) 163-179, and *Pilot study on the use of scientific literature by scientists*, by R R Shaw (National Science Foundation, 1956).

3 *Surveys*: of two main kinds, the oral interview and the written questionnaire. The oral interview can take two forms. Either questions are asked according to a pre-planned questionnaire (as in the BBC's audience research interviews) or the interviewer simply poses a number of general questions in order to get the subject talking. The advantage of an interview is that ambiguous points (which are found in even the most carefully planned questionnaire) can be resolved immediately. The written questionnaire should not be too lengthy, and the questions should be straightforward and, wherever possible, of the ' yes/no ' or multiple choice variety. Examples of studies based on questionnaires and interviews are numerous: a list is given on pages 21-42 of *Proceedings of the international conference on scientific information* as part of the report by E Törnudd which is based upon a questionnaire. M Slater *Technical libraries: users and their demands* (ASLIB, 1964) is a more recent investigation.

4

Other chapters are concerned with various aspects of meeting users' needs, as indeed is the entire field of dissemination of information. This section, therefore, is concerned with two very specific aspects: literature searching and the subsequent preparation of surveys and bibliographies; and the importance of external sources of information in meeting needs.

LITERATURE SEARCHING

The need for literature searches may arise in any kind of special library. They may be needed for marketing studies, for production planning or for policy decisions at management level, and commonly, for different stages in research projects. The latter can be illustrated as follows:

Stages in research projects	*Search needed*
1 Germination of research project from previous work or ideas	Current awareness
2 Definition of project, formulation of line of approach	Selective specialised *eg* ' What are the main current lines of research on lasers and which organisations are pursuing them?'
3 Detailed project planning, main lines of approach laid down, period of time to complete, finance, etc	Comprehensive specialised *eg* 'All available information on lasers as telecommunication devices.
4 Actual progress of research	Searches on specific problems as they arise *eg* properties of materials
5 Completion of and reporting on research	Verification of bibliographical references
6 Further research planning—another cycle	Further cycle of searches

Recent ASLIB research reported by M Slater (*op cit*) shows proportions for kinds of searches, the commonest being for ' description of object/process/method ', corresponding to stage four in the table above.

It must not be thought that literature searching is the sole prerogative of the librarian. Research shows that users are in fact more likely to do their own searches than rely upon library staffs. This is borne out in the report by Slater and by the following table

(I H Hogg and J R Smith ' Information and literature use in a research and development organisation ' in *Proceedings of the international conference on scientific information (op cit)* 131-162):

Number in status grade	6 research manager	57 senior grade	94 junior grade	157 overall
percentage of grade who:				
always did own search	0	14	31	24
sometimes did own search	33	75	64	66
never did own search	66	9	3	8
never needed search	0	2	2	1

The actual conduct of a search will vary according to the subject and the nature of the enquiry. For example, the technique for finding a piece of data is to go first to the standard data books in the appropriate subject and then to abstracts, which when informative, are important sources of such information. The technique for a complete bibliographic search can be outlined as follows:

1 Interview to determine the real needs of the enquirer. There are three main points to ascertain—subject scope, depth of the user's present subject knowledge, and period of time to be covered. It is usual to record these facts on enquiry forms designed so as to guide the interviewer. Examples of such forms can be found in L J Strauss and others *Scientific and technical libraries* (Interscience, 1964) chapter eleven.

2 Familiarisation with subject field through encyclopedias, and periodical articles.

3 Selection of bibliographical tools to be used.

4 Searching abstracting and indexing journals, beginning with latest available index and proceeding back in time. All relevant items should be noted on cards and a record should be kept of all headings and references which have yielded information. Where differences of terminology are found, previously searched sources should be rechecked. It will often be found that there are certain prolific authors, issuing bodies and journals in any one field, and therefore author indexes and corporate body indexes should be checked when the subject search has been completed; wherever

possible current volumes of cited journals should be checked for latest references.

5 Final check on library's own indexes and catalogues.

Further information on the conduct of searches is to be found in M Ciganik ' Scientific, technical and economic information in a research organisation' in *Proceedings of the international conference on scientific information (op cit)* 613-647; C W Hanson ' Subject enquiries and literature searches' ASLIB *Proceedings* 15 (11) November 1963 315-322; and H E Voress ' Searching techniques in the literature of the sciences' *College and research libraries* 24 (3) May 1963 209-212.

Final presentation of the results of a search may vary from simply handing over a file of cards to the enquirer to select the references he requires to the production of a bibliography or survey. For a bibliography the necessary steps are : 1 arrangement of entries in desired order; 2 editing entries; 3 preparation of any indexes; 4 composition of final copy; 5 reproduction and circulation.

Preparation of a survey necessitates reading all useful references and collating and presenting the information in a continuous form. This is often the most suitable method of presentation for the results of selective specialised searches or searches for economic information.

EXTERNAL SOURCES OF INFORMATION

No matter how generous a librarian's budget, it is inevitable that he will have to have recourse from time to time to sources of information outside his library. When considering external sources it is important to differentiate between those which can supply materials only and those which can supply information. Often the librarian knows from his bibliographical tools which books, periodicals etc he needs to satisfy a request. He frequently finds, however, that he is unable to trace information outside his own subject field since his bibliographical tools will be limited to some extent by the subjects covered by his collection. This is not to say that he will have no general bibliographies at his disposal, but that extensive bibliographical coverage of other subjects will be less likely. Under these circumstances the librarian must depend on external sources. Although it is difficult to categorise these sources accurately they fall roughly into two types; but it should be remembered that these are not watertight divisions and some sources could fit into both. They are: sources which can supply materials; and sources which can supply information.

Material sources: Into this category must obviously come the regional and national interlending system of which little need be said here. For those unfamiliar with the present system recommended readings are: P H Sewell *Library Association conference papers* 1962 35-42 and *Inter-library co-operation in England and Wales: report of a working party of the Ministry of Education* (HMSO, 1961).

Perhaps of greater significance to this paper are those other sources attempting to make special arrangements to cater for the needs of information workers in science and technology *eg* the National Lending Library for Science and Technology (NLL) and local schemes of co-operation.

The loans service of the NLL should be known, as well as the coverage of the library. It has been described often in periodicals *eg* D J Urquhart *Library Association record* 64 (9) September 1962 319-322. Note that the NLL cannot accept subject requests at all, but does have a system of local agents who, before appointment as agents, must satisfy the NLL that sufficient bibliographical tools are in stock to turn subject requests into requests for specific items. These requests for publications can then be sent to the NLL. In recent years there have been many special schemes of co-operation organised to cater for the needs of industry, usually based on a large public library. Of these the Sheffield interchange organisation (SINTO) is longest standing. There are many others, also referred to by their initials, *eg* TALIC, NANTIS, HULTIS etc. As most of these organisations will accept subject requests as well as requests for specific items, they could be equally well included in the later section on sources which will supply information. Many of these organisations have produced guides to resources within their own area (*eg* NANTIS *Handbook and directory of resources*), and most produce some literature descriptive of the service. When examining any of these schemes note the subject scope, libraries covered, co-operation with other sources, *eg* NLL, Science Museum Library, research associations. A most useful paper in relation to these schemes is N E Binns ' Co-operative schemes of library service for industry and commerce' UNESCO *Bulletin for libraries* 15 (6) November/December 1961, 310-316.

Information services: While the special librarian will use formal interlending services, he may also often use services offering much more information. Broadly these services can be divided into: research associations; trade associations; official government sources; societies and institutions.

Research associations: The job of the research association is to carry out research for the technical advancement of the industry which it serves. The results of this research are embodied in the association's reports. Technical meetings are arranged by research associations and the proceedings of these meetings are usually made available in report form or published for sale. Most firms are members of research associations which are of interest to them. Since associations are financed by members' subscriptions with the aid of government grants, it is not surprising that most of the information they produce is limited to member firms. To the librarians of such firms this information is freely available, except for highly confidential material. The information service given to members by research associations is usually excellent in quality and consists in supplying report literature (and sometimes that of other research associations) published information, and often confidential information gleaned from other sources. Librarians of member firms can obtain considerable help, particularly with difficult subject enquiries. Librarians of non-member firms may receive help direct or through a research association in a related field of which the firm is a member. The degree of assistance given to public bodies depends on the policy of the individual association concerned, but most will help whenever they can.

At least two research associations should be known in some detail. A list of associations can be found in DSIR *Research for industry*. Most associations issue annual reports which should be perused and any reports of the work of the information services traced through *Library science abstracts, Library literature* and abstracting and indexing services of the subject field of the association.

Trade associations: As with research associations the librarian of an industrial firm has valuable sources of information in the trade associations of which the firm is a member. Unlike a research association the object of a trade association is to look after the commercial interests of its members. Most employ staff to collect information on the industry itself, new developments, foreign competition etc and it is for this commercial information that the trade association is particularly valuable. Assistance given to public bodies and non-member firms is usually limited to that information which is generally available to the public *eg* published reports, general statistics concerning the trade, etc.

Official sources: It is sometimes difficult for an information worker in a particular field to discover the full extent of information available from official sources. Into this category of sources come government department libraries (*eg Board of Trade*); research station libraries (*eg National Physical Laboratory, National Engineering Laboratory*); national undertakings (*eg* NCB, CEGB, UKAEA, and those other national libraries such as the Patent Office Library). The degree of information available from them varies depending on the organisation. Thus the Patent Office will not lend books but will supply photocopies of periodical articles. The National Engineering Laboratory will not only lend material but will supply reprints of periodical articles, reports etc.

Many produce valuable reference tools (*eg* NEL *Heat Bibliography*). Most official agencies provide an information service and they are often an excellent source for translations, abstracts and information bulletins. Note that some government department libraries (*eg* UKAEA, Royal Aircraft Establishment) hold considerable files of confidential information which may or may not be available to others. Security classified information will only be released to those with the necessary security clearance. It is advisable to know, for the purposes of this paper, some information services of these official bodies. ASLIB *Directory* will reveal those of a given subject area and *Library science abstracts* will provide many references to descriptions of individual government libraries, *eg* J P K Pirie, ' The national engineering laboratory library ', SLA *News* 49 September-October 1961 9-11. Two specific libraries on which information should be gathered are the Patent Office Library, and the National Reference Library for Science and Invention (see *Journal of documentation* 17 (1) March 1961 1-39, and *Library world* 61 (720) June 1960 249-251).

Societies: One of the main functions of a professional society or institution is to provide an information service on the subject field covered by the society. In most cases the original intention was to provide this service for members only, but society libraries have now grown to such an extent that they are often looked upon as the main source of information in their subject field. It is to the credit of society librarians that most will attempt to satisfy requests either for specific items or subjects regardless of the origin of the request. Society libraries, many of which are of long standing, are rich in materials and often have exchange arrangements with kindred organisations in other countries. In a search for published information, the most likely source to try is often a society library. It is advisable to know the work of one or two societies, noting publications, library services, abstracting, translating, etc. *Library science abstracts* and *Library literature* will reveal many articles of use, *eg* M L Pearl ' The information and library services of the Iron and Steel Institute ' *Journal of the Iron and Steel Institute* 201 (4) April 1963 310-316.

Another frequently used source of information is that of direct approach to a personally known colleague for information which he is likely to have because of the subject interest of his parent organisation. There is nothing underhand about this system; it is done quite openly, most employers relying on the discretion of their information staff not to disclose confidential information. Often the experienced librarian can save time by a judicious use of this system. The inexperienced would, however, be well advised to use it cautiously at first as too many direct requests for materials which can be supplied perhaps more readily by conventional inter-lending facilities are irritating.

CHAPTER NINE: THEORY OF INFORMATION RETRIEVAL

INFORMATION storage and retrieval (*isar*) is a subject upon which a vast amount of literature has been published. It is, therefore, a field which can frighten the student by its size and complexity until he realises that in fact much of what is written is often either repetitious or redundant. Much describes abortive experiments, more merely describes systems (some never being heard of again) and this leaves little of real worth—and even less which can be described as theoretical.

To begin with it is necessary to approach isar theory from the point of view of the whole system. B C Vickery in *On retrieval system theory* (Butterworth, second edition 1965) has outlined the elements which make up an isar system and this outline is reproduced in diagrammatic form as figure four. Using this diagram it is possible to pick out the problem areas and view the present state of knowledge in relation to them:

1 *The documents*: it is probably an over-simplification to say that *all* retrieval problems stem from the original documents, but it is true that many do so. This is largely because of linguistic problems: if standard vocabularies were used in every field, if common inter-field terminology was also standardised, and if authors could be persuaded to give intelligible, descriptive titles to their work, some of the problems of isar systems would be removed. This problem of terminology and the growth of specialised vocabularies is well discussed by F Jonker in *Indexing theory, indexing methods and search devices* (Scarecrow Press, 1964).

2 *The analysis by the indexer*: the three items of information produced by the indexer are the 'specification' (*ie*, typically, a catalogue entry), the 'store address' (*ie* class numbers, report numbers or accession numbers depending upon how the store is arranged), and the 'descriptors' (*ie* terms used in subject analysis). Of these, the latter are the main subject of concern and two aspects can be emphasised:

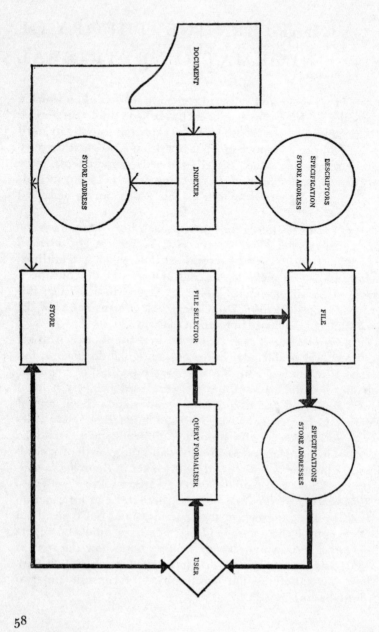

FIGURE FOUR: AN ISAR SYSTEM

a) The construction of descriptor languages, fully discussed by Vickery, and currently under investigation at Cranfield. Recent references include F W Lancaster and J Mills 'Testing indexes and index language devices' *American documentation* 15 (1) January 1964 4-13 and C W Cleverdon and others 'Uncovering some facts of life in information retrieval' *Special libraries* 55 (2) February 1964, 86-91.

b) The analysis of documents and selection of appropriate descriptors. This is an aspect of the problem which has received very little attention. Problems which arise include the skills of the indexers and their qualifications, consistency of performance, and aids to indexing. Some work on this has been done at Documentation Incorporated in the US, where it was found, predictably, that experienced indexers were more consistent than beginners. Further work showed that consistency is greater if indexers are told to index from particular parts of documents, and that improvement is found if indexing aids such as thesauri and classification schemes are used. Some of this work is reported by V Slamecka in *American documentation* 14 (3) July 1963 223-228. The ASLIB Cranfield Research Project seemed to indicate that indexing skills were more important than subject skills but this is a disputed topic and one which was not thoroughly tested at Cranfield.

3 *The organisation of the file*: this covers two topics—the physical collation of descriptors and specifications, and the internal structure of the relations between descriptors. For the first of these there are two possibilities: item entry and term entry. The commonest example of item entry is found in the card catalogue where the subject descriptors appear on the cards bearing the catalogue entries. Term entry is the reverse of this: each unit represents a descriptor and bears a record of all items to which that descriptor has been assigned. The commonest example of this is the UNITERM co-ordinate indexing system. All isar files are of one variety or the other whether they are ordinary card systems, punched card systems, mechanical or electronic systems. Most indexing languages attempt to show relationships between descriptors; one which does not attempt to do so is said to use 'bare' descriptors. Various methods of indicating relationships are used *eg* interfixing, the indication of relation by suffixing or prefixing symbols to document numbers; role indicators, which indicate the sense in which a term is used *eg* a chemical compound may be a

raw material, a product or a waste; and relational symbols, such as Farradane's analets. Generic relationships may be expressed either by cross references, as in an alphabetical subject catalogue, or by classification of terms with or without a notation. Vickery deals with this topic in depth in chapter six. Chapter two of *Methods of information handling* by C P Bourne (Wiley, 1963) and *Some fundamentals of information retrieval* by J R Sharp (Deutsch, 1965) are also useful.

4 *The organisation of the store*: this is not a problem of any very great importance. If the store of documents is available for browsing then some form of subject arrangement is desirable, but otherwise any searchable sequence will suffice.

5 *Query formalisation*: *ie* conversion of the enquirer's natural language question into the formal language of the isar system. Problems include: a) recognition of the enquirer's true problem; b) familiarity with the enquirer's terminology; c) conversion of the question into the system's language.

The last of these involves precisely the same problems as the initial indexing and the system may have aids such as a thesaurus for a co-ordinate indexing system or the subject index to a classification scheme. One of the few references on a) and b) above is 'Information retrieval, a view from the reference desk' by M Francillon, *Journal of documentation* 15 (4) December 1959 187-198.

6 *File searching*: the major task here is to devise a searching strategy appropriate to the organisation of the file. Vickery points out that 'successful retrieval is very far from being a simple matching of question codes against descriptor codes', but must include more inclusive terms, included terms, and related terms. C L Bernier in *American documentation* 9 (1) January 1958 32-41 illustrates the complexity of the situation by examining a number of hypothetical systems, *eg* a system with 10,000 documents, a vocabulary of 1,000 descriptors, each document being indexed by 10 descriptors. When searching such a system for a product of four descriptors, the chance of finding at least one relevant document is only five in 100,000. In real systems the chances are better but the theoretical figure illustrates the problem.

The remaining stages on the diagram, *ie* the selection of suitable references from those presented and the retrieval of documents from the store, are not topics which present real theoretical problems. Subjects which are of theoretical interest and which are concerned with the overall system expressed by the diagram include:

1 The purpose of isar systems, based upon the requirements of users—a subject which has received detailed investigation in certain organisations and subject fields (see chapter eight) but very little application to the kind of isar system required. The student would do well to think about this in relation to specific situations described in the literature.

2 The economics of different systems. Again very little hard factual information is available and different systems are often costed on different bases making comparison impossible. Articles which give some information on costs include ' Testing, comparison, and evaluation of recall, relevance, and cost of co-ordinate indexing with both links and roles ' by B A Montague, *Proceedings of the American Documentation Institute* 1964 357-367; ' Cost analysis and simulation procedures for the evaluation of large information systems ' by C P Bourne and D F Ford *American documentation* 15 (2) April 1964 142-149; and ' Indexing costs for 10,000 documents ' by L H Linder *Automation and scientific communication* (American Documentation Institute, 1963) 147-148.

3 The evaluation of the efficiency of isar systems. Here the key work is that done by C W Cleverdon and his colleagues at Cranfield and described in: *Report on the first stage of an investigation into the comparative efficiency of indexing systems* (College of Aeronautics Cranfield, 1960); *Report on the testing and analysis of an investigation* (Cranfield, 1962) and *Report on a test of the index of metallurgical literature of Western Reserve University* (Cranfield, 1963); and summarised in a number of periodical articles and in chapter nine of Vickery (*op cit*). Since the publication of the reports on the Cranfield Project there has been considerable interest in this field, with much disputation, and the student is advised to locate and read reviews of the Cranfield reports.

CHAPTER TEN: INDEXING IN SPECIAL LIBRARIES

THE term 'indexing' seems to defy definition, the difficulty being to distinguish between it and cataloguing. Within this syllabus, however, indexing means subject indexing—the subject description of documents, parts of documents, data, information and sources of information. It is closely related to subject cataloguing and indeed some writers use the terms synonymously. In special libraries indexing of periodical articles, reports, conference papers and even correspondence is commonplace, but neither is it unknown in general libraries; eg a public commercial and technical library may well maintain trade-mark indexes and indexes to local societies and sources of information. Within the information framework shown in figure four, indexing is the key operation in the 'input' stage and, following upon the analysis, results in the assigning of subject descriptors to documents.

Because of the number of systems described in the literature, the student may be forgiven for thinking that he has found his way into a morass of conflicting ideas. Conflicting ideas there are, it is true, but more confusion is caused by conflicting terminology. The student should school himself to recognise similar ideas regardless of the words used to describe them. The most useful general work for this part of the syllabus is B C Vickery *Classification and indexing in science* (Butterworth, second edition 1959); the same author's *On retrieval system theory* (*op cit*) is also useful, but the student should remember that no one work can cover all aspects, and should keep himself up-to-date with current reading. The semi-annual survey of literature on special libraries which appears in the *Assistant librarian* is useful in this respect. All indexing systems can be divided into two groups: those which employ natural language terms in an alphabetical sequence, as in alphabetical subject catalogues; and those which are arranged by the notational symbols of a classification scheme. This does not mean that there is no relationship between the two. Indeed it can be said that there are few alphabetical indexing systems into which classification does not enter at some point.

Alphabetical systems have certain basic problems which were first dealt with at length by C A Cutter, whose *Rules for the dictionary catalog* are still worth reading in this respect. The debate begun by Cutter is continued by J Metcalfe in his two works, *Information indexing and subject cataloging* (Scarecrow Press, 1957) and *Subject classifying and indexing of libraries and literature* (Angus and Robertson, 1959). Metcalfe is probably the chief protagonist for alphabetical subject indexes, and while his works are rather repetitious they are well worth reading.

Since Cutter's day the documents acquired in libraries, and particularly in special libraries, have come to deal with more and more complex ideas and more and more specific aspects of individual branches of knowledge. The subject heading RATS is probably good enough for a zoology textbook on this mammal, but more often today the indexer is faced with titles such as: ' On the action of hormones which accelerate the rate of oxygen consumption and fatty acid release in rat adipose tissue in vitro '. In this title the following terms have some significance for subject description: HORMONES: ACCELERATION: OXYGEN CONSUMPTION: FATTY ACID RELEASE: RATS: ADIPOSE TISSUE: and possibly ARTIFICIAL ENVIRONMENT rather than ' in vitro '. With documents of this kind, therefore, it is clear that the problem is not which ' subject heading' to choose from a list for subject description, but rather what combination of terms, of what specificity, in what order, and with what specification of relations which exist between them, and with other terms.

A number of writers have produced work on these problems. One of the earliest was J Kaiser, whose *Systematic indexing* (Pitman, 1911), when obtainable, is still worth reading. For those who cannot obtain it, or having done so find it difficult, a description is given in appendix J of Metcalfe's *Subject classifying* (*op cit*). Basically the system consisted of the recognition of ' concretes '— things in general and ' processes '—conditions of things, and the construction of headings by linking the two; *eg* BOOKS—BINDING; BIRDS—MIGRATION. This process was carried to the extreme of splitting terms representing compounds into the constituent concretes and processes; thus AGRICULTURE became LAND-CULTIVATION. The problem of combination of terms and word order in compound headings has been given considerable attention by E J Coates in *Subject catalogues: their headings and structure* (Library Association, 1960). Coates' ideas have found practical application in *British technology index* and the system is described in 'Aims and methods of the British technology index' by E J Coates *Indexer* 3 (4) Autumn 1963 146-152.

While relationships of some kinds can be expressed merely by the juxtaposition of terms, this becomes less satisfactory as the number of terms used in headings increases. This is so even when terms are used in a strict sequence according to some formula such as that of Coates. Some systems therefore, adopt prepositional phrases such as 'used in', 'effect of', 'for', and 'in' as *eg* FATTY ACID RELEASE—effect of HORMONES. An alternative is to analyse the kinds of relationships, and this has been done by J E L Farradane who uses symbols called 'relational operators' to combine terms ('isolates') into compound headings which he calls 'analets'. Farradane gives as an example of an analet the following:

Law/(British law/: [Cars/(Defects/: Accidents/;] Responsibility representing 'The law relating to responsibility for accidents arising from defects in cars in Britain'. Three operators are used in the above analet: /(—appurtenance, which includes relations of parts to wholes, /: —causation, and /;—association, 'the regular co-existence, expected regularly, of two experiences'. The relational operators are given a particular sequence and they therefore impose a particular structure, not only upon the terms in the headings but also upon the totality of headings in the file. Farradane has written a number of papers on his system, summarised in chapter nine of *Sayers memorial volume* edited by D J Foskett and B I Palmer (Library Association, 1961) and in D J Foskett *Classification and indexing in the social sciences* (Butterworth, 1963) 115-118.

A further problem in alphabetical systems is the expression of generic relationships through cross references—the problem being to construct a systematic network. Ever since Cutter it has been suggested repeatedly that this can be achieved by the use of a classification scheme. Coates (*op cit*) has taken this idea to the logical conclusion of deriving subject headings from classification numbers.

In recent years there have been many descriptions of co-ordinate indexing systems based upon Mortimer Taube's 'UNITERMS'—so called because of the use of single terms, thus FUEL ELEMENT is split into FUEL and ELEMENT. More recent systems use 'unit concepts' rather than UNITERMS and in that event the term FUEL ELEMENT would be used as it stands. The original manual method operates as follows:

1 Each incoming document is assigned an accession number and a number of UNITERMS.

2 Each term is assigned to a card with ten ruled columns, the accession numbers being 'posted' into the appropriate column by their final digit, thus:

FUEL									
0	1	2	3	4	5	6	7	8	9
	11		103			56		18	

3 Searching is performed by selecting the appropriate term cards and comparing the columns of numbers, common numbers indicating documents having the desired combination of terms.

The lists of terms used in co-ordinate indexing systems are referred to either as 'dictionaries' or 'thesauri' and at least one such thesaurus is commercially available. *Thesaurus of engineering terms* (Engineers Joint Council, 1964). An entry from this list is given below together with an entry for the same term from the US Bureau of Ships thesaurus:

EJC

Fuel cells
  BT Direct power generators
    Electric generators &
  RT Chemoelectric power
    generation
    Electric batteries
    Magnetohydrodynamic
    generators
    Solar generators
    Thermionic generators
    Thermoelectric generators

BuShips

Fuel cells
    (Voltaic cells that convert fuels
    eg H and O directly to electrical
    energy)
  Broader terms
    Batteries and components
  Related terms
    Electrolytic cells
    Energy conversion

It will be noted that none of the broader or related terms in the BuShips list are found in the EJC list, indicating very well the terminological hazards of alphabetical systems.

5

An interesting development in thesauri is typified by the *Eur-atom-thesaurus* (Euratom, 1964) in which the terms are not only listed alphabetically but are also presented in forty-two ' graphic display schemes ', each scheme presenting a related group of terms. The method of constructing such displays is given in ' The role of graphic display of concept relationships in indexing and retrieval vocabularies ' by L Rolling in *Classification research : proceedings of the second international study conference . . . 1964* (Munks-gaard, 1965).

Representative descriptions of co-ordinate indexing systems are given in ' The mechanics of co-ordinate indexing ' by J L Jolley ASLIB *Proceedings* 15 (6) June 1963 161-169 and ' Practical applications of " feature-card " systems ' ASLIB *Proceedings* 15 (6) June 1963 179-194. It is also discussed in most of the basic texts already referred to.

Classification schemes, traditionally, have been used for the arrangement of books on shelves and most of the major general classification schemes are ill-equipped to deal with documents such as research reports. There are two exceptions to this: UDC which was devised originally to deal with documents rather than books, and colon. Since the end of the second world war, and particularly since Ranganathan's idea of facet analysis has received attention from the Classification Research Group, many special schemes for limited subject fields have been produced. The detailed theory of classification is outside the scope of this paper, but the student should know how faceted classification schemes are constructed and should have a knowledge of one or two such schemes and how they are applied. Descriptions of the method can be found in the works by Vickery and Foskett already cited, and appendix B to Vickery's *Classification and indexing* gives examples of such schemes. *Faceted classification: a guide* by B C Vickery (ASLIB, 1960) is also a useful introduction. The use of UDC for indexing is discussed by Vickery in UNESCO *Bulletin for libraries* 15 (3) May-June 1961 126-138 and 147.

A classified index must have an alphabetical subject index as a guide. The now common method for constructing such an index is ' chain indexing ', originated by Ranganathan. It can also be used to construct alphabetical subject headings. Full description can be found in Coates (*op cit*) and in the other textbooks mentioned. During the testing programme of the Cranfield experiments, chain indexing was found to suffer from the particular defect that if a searcher was looking for a particular combination of terms, say B + F + K, this particular combination might be hidden in more complex combinations *eg* B + E + F + G + I + K, and useful information might be overlooked. In order to overcome this problem the ' cyclic ' or ' rotated ' index has been developed, and this is described in Foskett *Classification and indexing in the social sciences* (Butterworth, 1963).

Although not strictly subject indexes, ' citation indexes ' are significant in subject searching and, therefore, should be known about. The major service using this method is *Science citation index* but services are planned in other fields. Details can be found in *American documentation* 14 (3) July 1963 195-201 and in ASLIB *Proceedings* 16 (8) August 1964 246-251, but the idea can be quickly understood by looking at a fragment of a citation index:

SANDON IR	-------- 13 - J AM CHEM SOC	-------- 38	107
BECKER JA	J APPL PHYS	64 35	413
LAFFERTY JM	J APPL PHYS	E 64 35	426

This indicates that I R Sandon's paper beginning on page 107 of volume 38 1913 of the *Journal of the American Chemical Society* was cited by J A Becker on page 413 of volume 35, 1964 of the *Journal of applied physics* and in an editorial by J M Lafferty on page 426 of the same volume of the same journal. Thus the index can be used to search for related papers once a few references have been obtained.

CHAPTER ELEVEN: MECHANICAL AND ELECTRONIC METHODS

In this subject the student should have a grasp of the following:

1 The considerations upon which a decision to use machines must be based.

2 The elements of an isar system and their mechanisation.

3 The equipment for mechanised isar systems and representative examples of their use.

BASIC CONSIDERATIONS

The usual justification for trying to mechanise isar systems is the rate at which the output of scientific and technical literature is increasing and the failure of conventional systems to cope with the flood. Note however that this 'failure' is often assumed without much attempt to prove it, and in this respect Bar-Hillel's paper 'Is information retrieval approaching a crisis?' *American documentation* 14 (2) April 1963 95-98 is stimulating. Apart from this there are a number of design criteria that a machine system should ideally satisfy:

1 It should be capable of handling large quantities of information.

2 It should be superior, in economics and performance, to existing manual methods.

3 It should be capable of satisfying users' needs as and when they arise.

4 Arising out of 3 it should be accessible to a number of different users at the same time.

5 It should, therefore, be capable of being operated by all users without third-party intervention unless desired.

6. It should be possible to link the system into other existing systems.

No system which satisfies all of these criteria at present exists but the project at Massachusetts Institute of Technology under the direction of M M Kessler, see *Proceedings of the American Docu-*

mentation Institute (1964) 263-268, approaches them very closely and much theoretical work is being done elsewhere. For a stimulating forward look see *Libraries of the future* by J C R Licklider (MIT Press, 1965).

ELEMENTS OF AN ISAR SYSTEM AND THEIR MECHANISATION

Regarding figure four (page 58) as a model isar system, one can discuss its mechanisation from two points of view: its total mechanisation as a system, which has not yet been achieved, or mechanisation of certain elements. In this section the former will be emphasised, while the next section will consider the second.

Vickery, in *On retrieval system theory* (*op cit*), has broken down the isar system and discussed the requirements for its complete mechanisation. This section will therefore be devoted to the more problematical elements.

If a system is to be fully automatic this implies that the input operations must be performed automatically from the original documents, and for this there must be an efficient character reading device which can perform a scanning operation on text in order to transfer its contents to the machine's store. Otherwise the procedure must be done manually, which will add to cost and reduce efficiency. At present there is no sufficiently sophisticated character recognition device able to satisfy the requirements of an isar system, but research is proceeding apace and English Electric has announced a device which seems to be a big step forward, see *Science journal* 1 (1) March 1965 9-10.

The process of indexing involves a number of steps: analysing the document; selecting the appropriate descriptors; assigning specifications and store addresses. If these stages are to be performed entirely automatically, then the first step of manipulable text must be satisfied. For the present research is proceeding along a number of lines:

1 *Automatic methods of indexing*: early work in this field was done by H P Luhn of IBM, who based his work on the statistical analysis of words with the idea that the words which occur most frequently in a document are of most significance in subject description. It is now realised, however, that much more work is needed in the field of linguistics before automatic indexing can become a reality. A useful survey article is ' Mechanised document control' by F W Lancaster ASLIB *Proceedings* 16 (4) April 1964

69

132-152 and the USA National Bureau of Standards has published *Automatic indexing: a state of the art report* by M E Stevens (NBS Monograph 91, 1965).

2 *Automatic methods of deriving a classification scheme*: work is being done in this field both in England and the USA. In this country work is being done at the Cambridge Language Research Unit where the 'theory of clumps' has been evolved, built around a mathematical analysis of the co-occurrence of keywords in documents. The result of this analysis is something approximating to the classes in a classification scheme. In the USA, H Borko, at the System Development Corporation, is doing similar work. This idea is still in an embryonic state and the classification systems that have been derived are rudimentary and hardly yet suitable for practical application. It would appear, however, that it may be possible ultimately to derive classification schemes which are suitable for highly specialised collections of documents. Most writing in this field is difficult for the non-mathematician, but parts of Borko's paper ' Research in computer based classification systems ' in *Classification research (op cit)* 220-257 can be read with profit.

3 *Automatic methods of classifying documents*: defined as deciding mechanically to which subject field a given document belongs. Work on this is also being done by Borko and is referred to in the paper cited above. One of the problems is that as yet there is insufficient knowledge as to how *people* classify. Once this is known perhaps mechanical classification will proceed more rapidly.

The transfer of descriptors, specifications and store addresses to the file can be done automatically by a number of devices—key punches, tape typewriters, magnetic tape, or cameras, depending upon the nature of the file. If the previous steps have been carried out automatically this implies that the contents of the documents are already in the machine store and therefore transfer would be unnecessary.

Automatic searching procedures depend upon the nature of the file and various logical algebras, of which the commonest is Boolean algebra, have been adopted as searching logics. Full information on this will be found in *Textbook on mechanised information retrieval* by A Kent (Interscience, 1962) chapters four and five.

As an alternative to the total mechanisation of systems at some future date, there are those who would prefer the adoption of existing devices to do those tasks which can be mechanised now. For the student this demands a knowledge of the various devices and their application. An interesting collection of papers presenting this point of view is H Goldhor *(ed) Proceedings of the 1963 clinic on data processing* (University of Illinois graduate school of library science, 1964) which also includes a useful bibliography.

The chief devices used in mechanised isar systems can be divided into the following varieties: hand-punched cards; machine-punched cards; computer systems.

In addition there are a number of non-computer devices which use magnetic tape, paper tape and photographic film. All of these are thoroughly described, with excellent illustrations and diagrams in *Methods of information handling* (Wiley, 1963) by C P Bourne, while references to individual systems established since 1963 can be found in *Library science abstracts* or *Library literature*.

Hand-punched card systems: a) Feature cards or ' Peek-a-Boo ' cards are used to mechanise the UNITERM co-ordinate indexing system described in chapter ten. Instead of writing accession numbers on the body of the card, each card has a grid, each square representing an accession number, the appropriate position being punched on each ' term-card ' for a document. Searching is carried out by selecting the term cards, superimposing them over a light source and scanning for spots of light indicating documents with the terms in common. For descriptions of systems see the references in chapter ten and A Johnson ' Experience in the use of unit-concept co-ordinate indexing applied to technical reports ' *Journal of documentation* 15 (3) September 1959 146-155 and F Jonker ' The new " Termatrex " line of IR systems; the " Minimatrex " line of IR systems ' *American documentation* 14 (4) October 1963 276-282.

b) Needled cards may be punched or slotted on each edge as in the well known ' edge-punched ' systems or on the body of the card. These are described as needled-cards because searching is performed by passing a needle through those holes which represent search terms. Cards which have been punched in those positions drop out of the file. In some systems *eg* the Zator system the cards rest on rods slotted through the appropriate holes in a frame and thus cards which have been punched in the same position drop below the other cards in the file. Various coding systems exist for such systems and are fully discussed in Bourne (*op cit*) and in R S Casey and others *Punched cards: their application to science and industry* (Reinhold, second edition 1958).

Machine punched card systems: These use a variety of machines and cards are available in a number of different sizes, the commonest for isar applications being the 80 column card. The chief machines used are: a) the key punch, which looks like an elaborate typewriter. The operator depresses the keys to punch out the appropriate holes; b) the verifier, which is similar to the key punch and is operated in the same manner to check the original punching; c) the reproducing punch, with which cards can be duplicated, reproducing all, or any desired punchings; d) the sorter, which usually sorts by only one column at a time and therefore may require five passes to arrange a deck by five-digit numbers; e) the collator; which can select, merge or match cards.

Machine punched cards have been used to produce printed book catalogues, periodical holdings lists, and have a variety of other library applications. In addition to the works by Bourne and Kent already quoted, see also L J Anthony and J E Hailstone 'Use of punched cards in preparation of lists of periodicals' ASLIB *Proceedings* 12 (10) October 1960 348-360; M Griffin 'Printed book catalogs' *Revue de la documentation* 28 (1) February 1961 8-17; and E L Schulze 'An application of automation in the library: indexing internal reports' *Special libraries* 52 (2) February 1961 63-67.

Computer systems: in this part of the subject the student should know something about:

1 The general (very general) principles of computers and their operation. A useful work in this respect is *A simple approach to electronic computers,* by E H W Hersee (Blackie, 1959). The chief points to note are these: a computer consists of a number of elements: a) an input device—punched cards, paper tape, character recognition devices; b) a memory, most commonly a magnetic core, which contains the information in immediate use, supplemented by auxiliary memories in a variety of different media *eg* magnetic tape, and magnetic, random access discs; c) control units

—usually in the form of a push-button console to pass instructions to the rest of the system; d) a processing unit, which operates on the main memory, performing logical operations on the information in the memory; e) an output unit—printer, card punch, paper-tape punch, or oscilloscope display screen, illustrations of which can be found in *Bourne* (*op cit*).

In order to convert a task to computer operation it is necessary to describe the task in detail in the form of a flow-chart showing every operation; for details of this see 'Techniques of flow-charting' by L A Schultheiss in Goldhor (*op cit*).

Having flow-charted an operation, it is then necessary to translate the steps into machine language by 'programming'. There are a number of programming languages (FORTRAN, ALGOL etc) and the most recent are much nearer to natural language.

A further useful reference on the general principles of computers is *Special libraries* 51 (9) November 1960 485-492.

2 The varying capacity of memory, input, and output devices. Information on this can be found in J Becker and R M Hayes *Information storage and retrieval* (Wiley, 1963) chapter eleven, while briefer information can be found in *The present state of information retrieval by computer* by R C M Barnes, report no AERE-R 4514 (HMSO, 1964).

3 Searching techniques: already discussed above on pages 60 and 70.

4 Representative systems: computers are currently being used in a number of research projects and operational systems. Some of the research has been referred to already in relation to automatic indexing and classification. Operational systems include: permuted title or KWIC (keyword in context) indexes discussed in *Special libraries* 55 (3) March 1964 137-142; citation indexes, see previous references on page 67; computerised co-ordinate indexing systems *eg* 'Evaluation of co-ordinate indexing at the Naval ordnance test station' by M Bloomfield, *American documentation* 8 (1) January 1957 22-25; retrieval of legal information, see 'A look at research in legal information retrieval' by J F Horty in *Classification research* (*op cit*); the American Society for Metals/Western Reserve University Metallurgical Literature Searching Service, see *American documentation* 11 (2) April 1960 173-188 and 12 (1) January 1961 49-52; MEDLARS (medical literature analysis and retrieval system), see *The* MEDLARS *story*

(National Library of Medicine, Washington, 1963) and ALA *Bulletin* 58 (3) March 1964 227-230; and SLIC (selective listing in combination) in *Some fundamentals of information retrieval* by J R Sharp (Deutsch, 1965).

Notes on other systems can be found in the regular publication *Current research and development in scientific documentation* (National Science Foundation, Washington).

INDEX